Folklore Unbound

A Concise Introduction

Sabra J. Webber

The Ohio State University

WAVELAND
PRESS, INC.

Long Grove, Illinois

For information about this book, contact:
Waveland Press, Inc.
4180 IL Route 83, Suite 101
Long Grove, IL 60047-9580
(847) 634-0081
info@waveland.com
www.waveland.com

10-digit ISBN 1-4786-1533-8
13-digit ISBN 978-1-4786-1533-0

Printed in the United States of America

7   6   5   4   3   2   1

With gratitude for their support and encouragement, I dedicate this book to former Ohio State University Deans of Humanities Micheal Riley and John Roberts, to Dean of Humanities and Executive Dean of Arts and Sciences Jacqueline Jones Royster, and to the memory of Dean of Humanities Kermit Hall. Deans Extraordinaire all four.

Contents

Preface

There are many ways an introduction to folklore studies could be approached. I approach this one a bit differently from some very fine works that might serve as texts for an entire course on folklore. This is a short book; almost every sentence is meant to hint at a much longer conversation that would challenge glittering generalities about folklore and its disciplinary cousins. The work is meant for two different purposes and for people who are at different stages or places in their thinking or teaching about folklore.

The first purpose is, as the title implies, to introduce or expand on folkloristics for those in related fields who feel the pinch of the disciplinary tight chemise and want to see what else is out there. It could be used for research purposes or in an interdisciplinary seminar or history of ideas course covering the late modern to "postmodern" span of the twentieth century. The second use would be as the underpinning of a folklore course for which faculty would select supplementary readings in folklore or folkloristics fine-tuned to their own students' needs.

Because much of my work derives from field research outside North America, because more and more U.S.-trained folklorists are roaming far afield, and because I teach a course, developed with Katherine Borland, on "Global Folklore," I have drawn on cross-cultural examples that put diverse global locals in conversation. However, theoretical and methodological approaches introduced here derive very much from my training and subsequent work with(in) American folkloristics. As the title implies, I take an inclusive approach to folklore; in that sense, it should be taught early and often.

Finally, this book takes a small step toward introducing a diverse array of people who have worked with folklore materials over time—some of whom may be almost forgotten. As a folklorist, I am never happier than when I can refer to the creative and wise words of other folk. This book contains references to the insights of many folk, not all folklorists, but many more are to be sought out. Because we have been concerned with the creative lives of "others" throughout ages of imperialism, colonialism, neocolonialism, classism, and so forth, we must mediate between being frozen into inaction by fear of missteps in the delicate pursuit of understanding, or participating and thus always risking inadvertently contributing to the world's inequities.

Acknowledgements

Heartfelt thanks to Tom Curtin for his initial interest in my work and to my folklore colleagues Katey Borland and Patrick Mullen for their inspiring and insightful comments early in the writing process. Much appreciation to former departmental chairs David Horn and Dick Davis for their support for the project and especially to former dean John Roberts for pronouncing the book project "intriguing." Thanks to the Center for Folklore Studies at OSU, and especially Dorry Noyes, for arranging for me twice to present my work for comments and for all the folk who attended and made helpful remarks—especially Amy Shuman and Ray Cashman, as well as students from OSU and Indiana University. My colleague Margaret Lynd read the entire manuscript, and it was more than helpful to see *Folklore Unbound* from the perspective of a Pynchon scholar. My son, Alexander McDougal-Webber, who was an undergraduate student at the time, was a "test case" for the student (and activist) perspective and read and commented thoroughly on the initial chapters. Rachel Paiscik helped tremendously in pulling the bibliography together. All my best wishes go out to other scholars, including several who are or have been my students, who inspired me with their work and lives to think and write; many of you appear in this little book itself, and others are there in spirit—and in my library. Much appreciation goes to my colleague Julia Watson for her mentorship during the completion of the manuscript, and to Waveland editor, Jeni Ogilvie, a very talented editor who is also perfect to work with. Especially helpful at the final moment were the lively and insightful comments by Keith Walters, Susan Slyomovics, Dwight Reynolds, Carl Lindahl, Erika Brady and Sheila Bock. Finally, thanks to all my family, especially Ron and Stephanie, for their interest and encouragement.

Introduction
Folklore Today and Yesterday

Several tenets of folklore are inscribed in this book. Since disciplines change and adjust over time, this work is an overview of folklore not only as it now is but as it has settled into itself in the last 250 years. The book begins with an example from the lively folklore scene of the 1960s and 1970s, some one hundred years after folklore emerged as a "modern," "scientific," discipline. The following chapters trace important touchstones and paradigm shifts since those early days and look back at folklore and other new disciplines of the nineteenth century in order to hypothesize how we got here and how the roads less traveled might still affect future developments in folkloristics (the study of folklore). Scholarship in folklore has always intermingled with scholarship in the sciences, social sciences, arts, and humanities. The permeable nature of these (so-called) disciplines is evident throughout the book.

Many of the issues North American folklorists address today stem from the shake-up of the folklore scene beginning in the 1960s. That era of rethinking included (1) a refocus on folklorists themselves as members of multiple folk communities; (2) a reaction against earlier "othering," (marginalizing and thus silencing) of certain folk in our midst: Native Americans, women, the poor, and many more; and (3) resistance to the othering of those adversely affected by the domination of empire-builders or globalization. The latter include large categories of folk whose material culture and verbal arts were and are appropriated, sometimes for material or political gain, but sometimes

1

due simply to a careless disregard for the power differential that made such maltreatment almost inevitable.

An important figure in the 1960s reorientation of folklore studies is the late Alan Dundes, folklorist and gadfly who popularized the study of contemporary lore, like graffiti in bathrooms (he coined the phrase "latrinalia"), and photocopier lore. In the following example, Dundes chose to study the ritual behavior and verbal art of a folk community of college football players at UC Berkeley. The unofficial or folk "sayings" and practices that players develop and perform communally personalize the game, helping players and fans resist the tendency to turn college football into a business. Dundes could have focused on that dimension of football folklore without controversy but, instead, chose to address what football folk practices "reveal" about American masculinity.

A FOLK/LORE MOMENT

Alan Dundes was here . . . collecting Everyone knows that Alan Dundes doesn't do fieldwork It's true, I was just taking a crap. A. D.
> — Latrinalia exchange on the wall of the men's bathroom across from the Folklore Center at UT Austin circa 1977

In 1978, Alan Dundes, world famous as a folklorist in both popular and scholarly circles, published a short article, "Into the End Zone for a Touchdown," a psychoanalytic study of, according to his theory, homosexual elements woven into American football traditions. Dundes' folklore scholarship was frequently controversial, but the public outrage that followed the football article was extreme, rumored to have resulted even in death threats. On November 13, 1978, *Time* magazine referred to the controversy and quoted Ron Goldy, then a freshman football player at UC Berkeley, "I was so angry, I just wanted to get my hands on the guy—I mean on his neck."

Why all the controversy? Dundes was a folklore gadfly, and, despite the Disneyfication of folklore forms from belly-dancing to folktales, much of his work illustrates that folk practices, including those embedded in sports, are culturally relevant. They address issues that are almost certain to provoke controversy, divide communities, and underscore inconsistencies in cultural belief systems.

Unless "outed" by scholars like Dundes, folk practices often operate under the radar because their instigators are hard to trace (this is still true of written folk forms like graffiti and blogs). The content, from embroidery to tall tales, is dismissed by many participants as amusing or even compelling, but ultimately trivial. It is not, but the power of folk practices is often unnoticed by would-be censors. Thus, buried in the pageantry surrounding college football of the 1970s, communities brought together culturally contradictory masculinist "stories" within the protected frame of "play" or "game." When Dundes "innocently" speculated on the implications of these folkways, many passionate fans and footballers reacted angrily. They were shocked into an abrupt re-perception of folk traditions embedded in their game. In the late 1970s, when Dundes' article appeared, his homosexual tagging of the folk practices of football players, the manliest of men, was not simply dismissed as silly by players or fans; for some readers the details of "penetrating the end zones" of other men hit a nerve.

Since Dundes' intervention more than three decades ago, conversation about gender orientation and "proper" manliness has become more overt, even joked about, in popular culture. King Kaufman in "Football: America's favorite homoerotic sport" *Salon.com* (January 8, 2003), remarks, "The best TV commercial going during the playoffs is the . . . ad in which four collegiate-type guys watch a football game on TV together. They go to comical lengths not to touch each other—knees that accidentally meet jerk in opposite directions, hands that simultaneously land on a soda bottle recoil as though it were on fire. The camera cuts to a shot of the old alma mater scoring a touchdown on the tube, then back to the boys. They're having an orgy, rolling all over the couch, hugging for joy." Kaufman calls this commercial a "neat meditation on the repressed homoeroticism at the core of sports, and especially football, culture."

Lore itself is a useful resource for us, as members of various folk groups, to creatively address perspectives silenced or underrepresented in our culture. The *study* of folklore can be powerful, even dangerous, but potentially liberating to both the scholar and the community studied. Folklore studies can bring into public discussion complicated tensions and contradictions around homophobia, racism, sexism, classism, and other instances of injustice present even in some folk practices themselves. It takes time. Twenty-five years separate Dundes' article from this still edgy 2003 "orgy" ad in the realm of popular culture. In a 2010 Super Bowl ad, an obviously committed gay male couple is portrayed having a spat in their kitchen.

REORIENTING FOLKLORE

Despite global fame, prolific publications, and immense popularity as a Berkeley professor, Dundes was a curiously marginal, even maverick, figure in this marginal discipline, as folklore remains today. One of the so-called "young Turks," or rebellious American folklorists who were reinventing the field in the 1960s, Dundes never quite fit in with others of his generation, due partly to his light-hearted use of Freudian theory but also because of his cheeky disregard for propriety.

Yet, working from the periphery of the discipline, his scholarship resituated the field by encouraging young folklorists to attend to the history of the discipline through study of its own scholarly "ancestors" and those from nearby fields. Dundes opened up possibilities for scholarship for both popular and academic audiences, but especially for his students, in several directions: He expanded definitions of "folk" and "lore"; he underscored why lore should be studied both ethnographically (in context) and aesthetically (as texture); and he supported and inspired folklore fieldwork worldwide (while avoiding doing any himself).

THE FOLK

Dundes' chapter, "Who Are the Folk?" (1980), introduces folklore to a wide audience both outside academia and among undergraduates from all majors. It was critical in radically changing perceptions in North America of "folk" from "others" (rural, poor, ethnic, minority) to "all of us." By assuming that all of us are "the folk" and publishing articles like "Folk Ideas as Units of World View" (1972) he gave college students coming to Berkeley from all over the world new ways of thinking about their own folk culture(s). Conversely, each year, hundreds of students were sent out to do fieldwork assignments on folklore within their own familiar worlds—with their families, religious organizations, sororities, political associations, and, yes, their sports teams.

THE LORE

Inevitably, opening up the accepted definition of "folk" expanded what counts as "lore." It became difficult for lore to be peddled or plundered by folklore scholars (and artists) as romantic, anonymous, mystical, communal productions, survivals from the preindustrial period. Lore now includes contemporary practices in which we all engage. Dundes introduced, for example, the written lore of small groups—like "latrinalia" or photocopy lore—that led to the early recognition of Internet lore. His work segued with that of scholars in other disciplines who, in the 1970s, "studied up"—that is examined the culture of power, not just of the disadvantaged— and studied closer to home, investigating their own folk groups' lore.

The anthropologist Laura Nader (1974[1969]), for example, "studied up": she addressed the anthropological implications of proliferating nuclear power plants, and she conducted, as did Dundes, ethnographic studies of lawyers. Erving Goffman (1981), the sociologist, "brought it all back home" (Berreman 1972) by unpacking—closely analyzing the details (of)—scholarly events such as the lecture. A decade earlier, in science studies, Thomas Kuhn (2012[1962]) had "studied up" in his examination of how small-group, informal gatherings of scientific folk could lead to scientific revolutions, in a manner easily recognizable to a folklorist.

Inclusive definitions of folk and lore, the study of folklore in a global setting, folklore scholars' attention to the human sciences, and consideration of the aesthetic dimensions of lore became new emphases that made folklore relevant to contemporary cultural and social issues. At the same time, these new emphases ensured continuity with the past—tradition and/as change. Thus, Dundes underscored the power of folklore as a resource for us not only to understand the past in more complex ways but to comment on the present, as in the football example, and to prescribe for, anticipate, the future by drawing on a wide range of media and aesthetic forms.

BOOK PLAN

In the following chapters we look at the power and possibilities of folklore and folkloristics. Shifting ways of thinking about "folk" and "lore" affect both ethnographic and aesthetic approaches folklorists take to studying informants and their expressive culture. Moreover, along with political realities, ethical considerations guide changing choices about who folklorists study, where and what they study, and which disciplines they call on in terms of methods and theory. How folklorists can best "translate" their understanding of a particular folk and lore to others is vitally important.

Chapter 1, "Beginnings," investigates the emergence in Britain of the contemporary discipline of folkloristics. It begins with forces in the eighteenth and nineteenth centuries that coalesced around noticing various sorts of communal expressive culture: folktales and myths, ballads and dances, magic and religious rituals and festivals, and even sporting events. Notice was taken of vanishing customs that were considered quaint when found in the Western European countryside but were perceived as heathenish and shocking when seen in the rest of the Empire—in colonized locals. We will see that folklore is intertwined with other emerging disciplines, as well as scientific, political, and economic focuses of the time. Each section contains perspectives of one or two interesting thinkers who made that early period engaging.

Chapter 2, "Modern or Postmodern" takes a step back to look at some of the concerns that scholars in their various disciplinary pigeon-holes have shared with their cohorts in related fields. Although the grand narrative about our joint wanderings over the last two-hundred-plus years is considered, the focus is more on loci where we are still today grappling with issues similar to those of our scholarly ancestors. We share with them *dis*-ease, centering on humanistic concerns that are not easy to resolve.

Chapter 3, "Aesthetic Discourse and Cultural Affect," considers the "stuff" of folklore—what it is or isn't, its shifting contours. The chapter is divided into two parts: Part One considers the meaning of lore and the decades-long focus on verbal arts and related genres; Part Two is dedicated to the divergent path that material culture took on its way to becoming studied folkloristically.

Chapter 4, "Folk Soul and Primitive Mind," addresses the thorny issue of how folk communities have been engaged with (or ignored) over the last three hundred years. Although we still have much to learn, we know opportunities are missed if we do not remain connected to folk artists and their lore. This chapter looks at relations folklorists have had with their folk consultants and begins to identify the ethical challenges of working in this field.

Chapter 5, "Performance," considers folklore as necessarily performative. To understand the powerful potential of lore it is centrally important to recognize how much about communal life can be artfully ensconced in comparatively brief moments of fellowship. Here is where issues arising in other cultural domains (economic, social, environmental, and so on) are brought together and managed aesthetically.

Chapter 6, "Comparative Folklore," examines comparative dimensions of folklore, various approaches to the study of lore that since the beginning have been a counterpoint to folkloristic's sometimes nationalistic tendencies, and today potentially a powerful resource for putting locals (imaginings and representations of any particular here and now) in conversation in creative and mutually productive ways—opening up possibilities for "conversations" that draw on lore to effectively challenge loci of hegemonic power. Years ago I brought a student to my university from Turkey, now Professor İpek Çelik, who wanted to study comparatively Turkish and Greek playwrights who were embedding social commentary in contemporary drama. These groups addressed shared political concerns that resisted the molding or defining of their art by their respective nation states wherein a central focus would be Greek-Turkish enmity rather than issues within their own borders (Çelik 2002). These kinds of comparative projects have yet to reach their full potential.

Chapter 7, "Challenges for the Future," takes a brief look at what seems to be coming up for folklore and the disciplines in the near future. As this book is an introduction to folkloristics, I imagine that some readers are looking for ways to incorporate folklore into their own life's work or to become folklorists themselves. This final chapter discusses issues that are central to folklore studies today. The field has become edgier than ever in its efforts to support social justice while insisting on the central place of expressive culture in achieving justice goals.

Chapter One

Beginnings
Folklore Undisciplined, 1760–1900

Indeed, there is a sense in which significance inevitably lies in what things become, for it is the retrospective light that picks them out at all.
— Marilyn Strathern, "Reproducing Anthropology"

Folklore has been called the disciplinary "bastard begat upon English by anthropology." So folklorist Tristram Coffin (1968: v) summed up the generally held belief about the origins of this new discipline. Yet, anthropology and folklore studies evolved at almost the same time, in the last half of the nineteenth century. A modern language curriculum, including English, was not introduced at Oxford University until 1887, a bold move that had one prominent professor observing that Oxford was "about to reverse the renaissance" (Leerssen 221). Folklore was one of many emerging cultural focuses for the intelligentsia that were built around the political, scientific, religious, technological, and economic concerns of the Industrial Revolution of the late eighteenth and nineteenth centuries.

In Britain, those studying the "folk" or "lore" tended to be gentry—most not wealthy, but with connections and resources enough to pursue academic or artistic pursuits. Many were self-educated and most had multiple interests—literary, scientific, political—and thus belonged to more than one scientific or literary society or institute. Women were not entirely excluded. For example, in the late nineteenth century Lady Augusta Gregory, an ardent Irish nationalist, conducted fieldwork and published Irish folklore. She also wrote and produced plays, as well as immersed herself in local and global politics, early on defending Egyptian efforts toward independence from England.

8

Today, scholars are typically credentialed by their university affiliations, but in Britain at that time a long string of initials often followed lecturers' or authors' names to affirm their disciplinary authority. F.R.G.S. indicated a Fellow of the Royal Geographical Society, and F.R.A.I., the Royal Anthropological Institute. Folklorist Laurence Gomme, not uncommonly, belonged to a whole range of learned societies and institutes. As universities created more disciplinary departments in the twentieth century, folklore studies found a home in English and anthropology departments; indeed, folklore is sometimes incorporated as the fifth field in anthropology (cultural, physical, and linguistic anthropology; archeology; folklore).

Yet, until the end of the nineteenth century, folklore remained undisciplined, although institutes for both anthropology and folklore were established in Britain by the 1870s. Perhaps because of this lack of place in an academic hierarchy, interest in folklore in the eighteenth and nineteenth centuries was shared by thinkers in a wide variety of fields. Linguists, historians, psychologists, anthropologists, students of religion, biologists and geographers, as well as missionaries, nationalists, artists, soldiers, and diplomats all found the "stuff" of folklore compelling and drew on it to shed light on their own work.

Sigmund Freud, in his psychoanalytic investigations, and Johann Gottfried Herder, in his philological research, depended heavily on folklore. In turn, scholars of folklore mingled data, research tools, and analytical constructs from a variety of fields. Scientific, literary, and artistic methodologies used to study canonized works of art, literature, or music were adapted for the analysis of folktales, folk dance, rituals, festivals, drama, folk music, and even material culture items like religious monuments or house types. For example, while philologists borrowed folklore to support their ideas about the linguistic and affective (artistic, expressive) basis of nationalism, folklorists borrowed methodologies from linguists, biologists, and naturalists to classify folk practices by region and to trace their origins over time. They sifted through the memoirs and reports of missionaries and colonial government officials, studying them through the lens of folklore scholarship.

From the start, the broad scope of folklore has given it a slippery, trickster-like character, making it one of the most interdisciplinary of disciplines. Indeed, distinguishing the folklorist from the nonfolklorist remains challenging, as Steven Zeitlin illustrates in "I'm a Folklorist and You're Not" (2000). Definitions of folk and lore remain elusive, and definitions of who qualifies as a folklorist and what theoretical tools they might draw on continue to be debated.

This interdisciplinary scope and familiarity with a wide array of theoretical tools remains crucial to folklore studies. Folklore scholars continue to engage in direct, extended contact with groups, in each group's own communal contexts, as do ethnographers, anthropologists, linguists, and sociologists. At the same time folklorists foreground the performative aspects of the communities they study, as do scholars of art, music, drama, crafts, and so on. However, few artists or intellectuals in the eighteenth and nineteenth centuries were interested in how the folk (not then defined as "all of us") used their own lore. Instead, they collected lore to use outside of its communal context—for language study, as support for nationalist or colonialist aspirations, or for poetic or literary inspiration. Thus began a long history of scholarly cherry-picking of items of lore, often without attending to their localized meanings or to the intentions of their creators.

Over the last 250 years we find woven through studies of what would come to be called folklore two enduring, divergent strands that can be traced to the impact of the industrial age on Western Europe: first, a focus on the affective dimensions of culture that bind communities together, and, second, the desire to be considered modern and engaged in research rooted in scientific methods, a desire shared by most nineteenth-century intellectuals, whatever their objects of inquiry. Over the years folklorists leaning toward the affective have been criticized for being too "romantic," too engaged with a particular folk community or its festivals, quilts, dances or epics; at the same time, those leaning toward the scientific have been criticized as being "too cerebral" or too removed from the folk "under" study.

Two other early tendencies contributed to the internal debates that fueled the emerging discipline. "Armchair" scholars brought together written sources (either notes from the field or information culled from various books and manuscripts). They compared folklore from multiple regions of the world, while "field researchers" collected and analyzed their own data from more limited venues. Of the latter, some remained close to home while others traveled far afield, working intensively and learning the languages of a few particular corners of the world.

A CAUTION

Although serious, systematic study of folklore in Europe begins with the emergence of disciplines during the Industrial Revolution, communal expressive culture (folklore), of course, was not new. It had been noticed, valued, collected, studied, and shared for thousands of years by people across social classes and cultures. Yet, folklore was not disciplinarily marked off as communal aesthetics. In the Muslim world today, for example, the term *adab* simply means "literature," but in the medieval period it had a broader meaning, encompassing everything a well-bred, urbane, person should know. That knowledge included various genres of what we now call folklore, such as verbal art and customs like proper dining etiquette.

Sometimes items of lore constituted part of a high art tradition; in some regions of the world, a cultivated person was expected to know not only science and philosophy, poetry and religion, but also certain genres of verbal art—oral poetry and proverbs, for example, or folk music. Puppetry in medieval and early modern Egypt was sometimes defined and studied as "high art," if the Egyptian caliphs bestowed their patronage, and other times as "street theater"—relegated by the elite to the "other"—to the masses or the peasants.

Sometimes the status of what we now call lore was foregrounded and debated. The great sociologist of the fourteenth century, Ibn Khaldun, championed North African oral epic, challenging scholars who rejected it as artistically inferior to written works. More often, items of lore trickled down or up within or between culture groups, seemingly without much notice. For example, during the Ancient Roman Empire, North African Berber nannies told folktales to their Greek or Roman charges, and these stories seem to have woven their way into Greek and Roman "high art." Traveling merchants acquired stories, songs, riddles, and jokes to share and trade (as "affect capital," to put it crassly) along routes stretching across China to India, across the Indian Ocean to the Arabian Peninsula and the Mediterranean, or up from Africa, across the Sahara, and over to Spain.

Verbal artists, as well as dancers, singers, and musicians, male and female, entertained kings and emperors, as well as commoners in workplaces, coffee houses, and public squares. Then as now, artisans crafted carpets, pottery, and swords—such material culture resources were often kept alive through apprenticeships. Artful dimensions of local hawking, hunting, and fishing practices were communally shared over generations. Study of this earlier, perhaps less self-conscious, lore is fascinating, but outside the scope of this book project.

THE THEME OF LOSS

By the eighteenth century Western intellectuals experienced a sense of longing for the past and felt a need to acquire information about other cultures' (home or abroad) expressive practices. This drive to understand others was not simply aimed at perfecting trading or colonizing projects. At least some Europeans clearly harbored a suspicion that other cultures, like India or Tahiti, or other subculture groups, like gypsies, possessed knowledge that the industrializing West lacked or was losing. Lady Gregory relates in her autobiography a conversation with the great comparative philologist/folklorist

Max Müller, noting that he "still has a hankering for India" (Gregory 1976: 172). She quotes Müller's book, *India*, in which he writes that, although we call Indian notions of life dreamy, unreal, and impractical, they may look on ours as "short sighted, fussy and in the end most unpractical" (qtd. in Gregory 1976: 207).

Despite received wisdom that the Empire of the West felt itself at the top of the evolutionary ladder, we find such sentiments that suspect the contrary embedded in the works of folklore collectors, and these sensibilities still linger in folklore studies today. Folklorists often seek in the folk practices of others what seems to be lacking in their own, and, as environmentalists lament the extinction of species, many folklorists decry the loss of cultural diversity and local knowledge in a "modern," centralized, uniform, "Western" lifestyle.

THE FIRST FAKELORE OR THE HOMER OF SCOTLAND?: JAMES MACPHERSON'S OSSIAN

They came forth to war, but they always fell.
— James Macpherson, *The Poems of Ossian*

But Doctor Johnson, do you really believe that any man today could write such poetry? Yes. Many men. Many women. And many children.
— Samuel Johnson, *Lord Auchinleck's Fingal*

When I was a small girl in San Leandro, California, my mother showed me a secret sign that was used to toast Bonnie Prince Charlie, the eighteenth-century Scottish pretender to the British throne who was exiled to Italy in 1746, after losing the Battle of Culloden (in Scotland) to the English House of Hanover. The sign consisted of raising one's glass (of milk in my case), and, responding to a toast "to the king," passing the glass over one's water glass, thus secretly signifying that you meant the "king over the water," exiled in Europe. The massacre at Culloden and the subsequent brutal suppression of the Highland Scots had signified the forcible end not only of the Scottish clan system and much of Scottish culture, but of the Gaelic language itself.

In the mid-eighteenth century, the young Scottish poet James Macpherson returned from wandering in remote Highlands of Scotland with what he claimed were third-century Gaelic-language manuscripts, recordings of fragments of poems that a warrior and bard named Ossian recited when he was old and blind. By 1760 Macpherson had published *Fragments of Ancient Poetry*, and a year later he published (purportedly) Ossian's most famous epic, "Fingal" to wild international acclaim.

This enthusiastic reception of Ossian in that emotionally charged historical moment was matched by attacks on the poem's authenticity. English man-of-letters Samuel Johnson condemned the work as fake and bad poetry, as the quotation above makes clear.

Nevertheless, the epic, widely translated, spread quickly to Europe and the Americas reinforcing ideals of the romantic era: heroic struggles against oppressors; literary historicism as a means to recover the past; respect for rich oral cultures and less privileging of Greek and Latin ancient literatures; and the power of nature. Poets, writers, and artists of the Romantic or Primitivist schools were inspired by the Ossian epic. And, it encouraged nationalistic fervor rooted in love of native soil as well as in peoples' ancient, shared languages, especially where their losses was feared as in some Germanic lands.

Ironically, as Gaelic was being replaced by English in Scotland, Macpherson's work was published in English. (Macpherson claimed to have found manuscript fragments in Gaelic, but few were ever seen.). Subsequent debates over the work are important early indicators of folklorists' concerns with issues of "authenticity" or "purity" and with translation and "genre." The Macpherson episode also foregrounded two contradictory concerns: issues of domestication (making familiar) versus attempts to instill an exotic feeling (making strange, *ostranenie*) through translation in a "folk(sy) dialect."

FOLKLORE STUDIES AND THE NATION-STATE

Scotland has given us a Homer who does not chatter on and on, who is never coarse or monotonous, but rather simple, quick, precise and uniform yet at the same time varied.

— Cesarotti (qtd. in Leerssen's "Ossian and the Rise of Literary Historicism")

The Ossian epics inspired Europeans to collect their homelands' native oral literatures, thus providing an important impetus for the folklore "habit." Before the eighteenth century was out, translations of the Ossian poems served as inspiration for the formation of national identities. Finnish, Italian, Irish, and German folk, among others, would collect folk narratives (epics, but also ballads, folktales, and myths) of an earlier, supposedly linguistically unsullied cultural past to be embraced as "authentic" voices of the ancestors and the foundations around which aspiring nations needed to construct unique identities and histories. The Ossian epic confirmed for the German philologist Friedrich von Herder his own idea that nations emerge organically from the land,

languages, and literatures of a people. He collected folk songs to determine what was uniquely German. Inspired by Herder, the brothers
Grimm collected German folktales, believing them to be, like Ossian's
poems were for the Scots, the roots of their culture.

POPULAR ANTIQUITIES VERSUS MANNERS AND CUSTOMS: "SURVIVALS" AND THE BIRTH OF FOLKLORE

Use "popular antiquities" as a library search term and the results
will reveal references back to about the mid-1700s, often coupled with
terms like "curiosities," "vulgar," "provincial," and "superstition,"
depending on the decisions of cataloguers. A library search under
"survivals" yields results beginning in the mid-nineteenth century.
"Folklore," the term that caught on when proposed in 1846 by the
English collector William John Thoms, largely replaced other English
labels by the twentieth century.

As in the case of the Ossian epic, popular antiquities were
"discovered"—noticed by Western intellectuals—surviving among
rural, unlettered populations. Urban intellectuals and artists theorized that these folk embodied the spirituality that others had lost
due to industrialization; they believed that they were closer to
nature, possessed innate talents for music and dance, and displayed
an attractively rough poetic nature unsullied by the Industrial Age.

The romantic poet William Wordsworth, a contemporary of
Macpherson, was widely acknowledged to have been influenced by
the Scot, while disdainful of him and his admirers. Wordsworth's
poem, "Ode: Intimations of Immortality from Recollections of Early
Childhood," conveys the loss of the mystical and earthy connections
of innocent children and peasants that are left behind as a person's or
a civilization's childhood comes to an end.

> What though the radiance which was once so bright
> Be now for ever taken from my sight,
> Though nothing can bring back the hour
> Of splendour in the grass, of glory in the flower,
> We will grieve not, rather find
> Strength in what remains behind;
> In the primal sympathy
> Which having been must ever be;
> In the soothing thoughts that spring
> Out of human suffering;
> In the faith that looks through death,
> In years that bring the philosophic mind. (1804[1940]: lines 180–191)

Wordsworth and artists like the painter Paul Gauguin or the novelist Sir Walter Scott drew on their artistry to temper the harsh realities of industrialization.

Closely linked to this urban, industrialized citizen's sense of loss was a popular interest in spiritualism, as both scientists and artists attempted to reconnect with friends or loved ones beyond the grave. Starting in New York in the mid-1800s the spiritualist movement grew to have an estimated eight million followers, the largest numbers in the United States and Britain. With the advent of the modern age in the late nineteenth century, though, such practices were widely criticized by the "scientifics," who became disaffected as instances of fraud were uncovered.

SINGING, DANCING THRONG: THE COMMUNAL OR "MARSHMALLOW" THEORY

Cultural evolutionism—the theory that all cultures move through stages from savagery to barbarism to civilization—was already one (among other) commonly accepted theory of cultural change in the eighteenth century well before Darwin's 1859 account of evolution in *Origin of Species*. Nevertheless, the new scientific disciplines of the late nineteenth century, particularly analogies between biological and cultural evolution and Freud's claim that cultural evolution paralleled stages from child to adult, reinforced theories of cultural evolutionism, lending them scientific credibility.

Emerging fields of botany, geology, physiology, and geography exhibited two common tendencies that Darwin's work and the global spread of European colonialism reinforced and enabled. The first, mentioned above, was the impulse toward classification and mapping of flora, fauna, and geological formations—but also of human characteristics like body types, languages, ethnicities, and races. In the realm of what would later be called "folklore," differences and similarities among various material culture items such as pottery, as well as folktales, myths, religious practices, ballads, and dance, were mapped and classified.

The second tendency reinforced by Darwinism was foregrounding the past and the fascination with tracking change over time. Layers of the past could be found in the study of geological phenomena or of flora and fauna. So, too, could traces of the past be discerned in the study of the present-day social life of "barbarians" or "peasants." The theory was that European rural cultures and "primitive" or "savage" non-European cultures retained traditions surviving from earlier stages that simply weren't needed in contemporary times, just as people have vestigial organs (like the appendix) that were thought to have served a purpose in an earlier evolutionary stage.

Darwin's theory, with its focus on biological origins and stages of development, gave weight to this hypothesis of a similar evolutionary process of cultural "progress" from primitive to savage to civilized. Study of such behaviors still found among barbarians and peasants (and children) would allow for the reconstruction of human social development over time, just as the bones of extinct animals provided information about biological evolution.

In this context, most Western intellectuals did not consider the "folk" responsible for creating their dances, religious practices, ballads, folktales, myths, and legends, nor did they believe the folk to have analytical insights into their own practices. Rather, many scholars believed this valuable cultural material was produced communally, without conscious authorship, since they considered the folk less mentally "evolved" than their urban, educated contemporaries. If today we are all the folk, we weren't then. Most students of folklore did not consider that the folk included individual men and women with the acute observational skills necessary to comment thoughtfully on the human condition. As Joseph Leerssen observes, scholars like Lonnrot, the "Finnish Grimm," producer of Finland's national epic, the *Kalevala*, and Jacob Grimm himself supposed "that folk poetry was virtually authorless, that it 'wrote itself' and was an outgrowth of the nation's collective experience" (2004a: 238). Across Europe in the eighteenth and nineteenth centuries it was widely held that oral poetry provided the raw materials from which literary epics emerged.

As we see from the quotation above by Cesarotti, who translated the Ossian epic into Italian in the 1760s, it was Scotland itself that produced the Scottish Homer. During this period, then, folklore constituted, with rare exceptions, specimens to be collected and studied separately from the people among whom those materials were found. Communally created, these rough folk creations could inspire writers like the German Goethe or Macpherson himself to write grand fiction or paint powerful works of art celebrating the native landscapes in which they felt rooted.

Although scholars generally agreed on the organic and communal origins of lore in a "singing dancing throng," a phrase attributed to the early twentieth-century scholar Francis B. Gummere, they disagreed over the degree to which oral versions of ballads and folk narratives should be "improved" by scholars. For ethnographers today, representation of lore continues to be a difficult challenge. Nevertheless, the "improvements" early collectors made to their informants' materials—whether to find a larger audience, make the material suitable for children, correct presumed "faults" their collectors thought had crept in over time from some imaginary original, or make them sound more or less folksy—are not acceptable to contemporary Western folklorists.

While alterations to lore continued into the twentieth century, scholars who respected the creativity of individual folk gained ground. By the early twentieth century, folklorist MacEdward Leach mocked communal theory as "the marshmallow theory," lore composed while everyone sat around a bonfire toasting marshmallows (Alvey 1973: 82). At the same time lore was still assumed by most to consist of simpler forms from which "elite" artists could draw inspiration for their symphonies, operas, literature, sculpture, paintings.

EARLY FOLKLORE STUDIES:
MRS. GRUNDY & FLUTTERING IN THE DOVECOTES

Whether . . . the cult be barbaric or civilized, we find theory and practice identical. The god is eaten so that the communicant thereby becomes a "partaker of the divine nature." . . . There is only the need to point out that the inclusion of the rite within the province of folklore is warranted by its identity with barbaric rites.

— Edward Clodd, 1896 Presidential Address, Folk-Lore Society

By the early nineteenth century the rigidity and repressiveness of British society, the fear of censorship, whether by law or straitlaced public opinion, was personified and named "Mrs. Grundy" after a censorious character in an English play. As might be expected from the example of attacks on Alan Dundes mentioned earlier, students of folklore like the late-nineteenth-century president of the British Folklore Society, Edward Clodd, also a London bank officer and free-thinker, were among those who fell afoul of Mrs. Grundy.

A friend of Charles Darwin and other "scientifics," in 1896, Clodd expounded in his second presidential address on how various religious customs, like Holy Communion, were leftovers from ancient pagan practices. The speech caused, as folklorist Sona Burstein (1957) later put it, "fluttering in the dovecotes." Uproar ensued, listeners stomped out, members of the Society resigned, including former Prime Minister William Gladstone, and the Catholic Church wrote a twenty-four-page protest against Clodd's "assault on Christianity." It is evident that at least some folklorists of the time did not think their own lives had a folk dimension (or, if it did, they should resist it).

In his first, less controversial presidential address to the Folk-Lore Society in 1895, Clodd mentions a friend and fellow victim of Mrs. Grundy, the author Thomas Hardy. It might be surprising to draw on a novelist to examine popular antiquities studies, but as the late American folklorist and historian Richard Dorson wrote of British rural studies of that time, "rarely did the collector venture into the field for any extended time" (1961: 308). Hardy did, living as a participant observer among the people about whom he wrote.

To founders of the British Folklore society, Hardy was an informant, but as a novelist, he shared his insights with readers and with researchers in multiple fields—philologists (Herder and the Grimm brothers), cultural historians, scholars of myth and ritual (Max Müller, Sir James Frazer, Andrew Lang), archeologists (Augustus Pitt Rivers), and philosophers (Auguste Comte, Herbert Spencer). In 1894 Hardy wrote to Clodd, "Every superstition, custom, etc. described in my novels may be depended on as true records of the same" (qtd. in Zeitler 2007: 21). Hardy's work, from the point of view of folkloristics, brings together a number of early characteristics that continue to define the discipline. He relied on the folk lives of his home village to lend verisimilitude to his novels—so much so that his work approaches ethnography—with benefits.

Hardy created a fictional rural English community, Wessex, that he intended to be ethnographically sound and to include many of the expressive dimensions of the region—an array of genres that he knew intimately, from seasonal ritual to storytelling. While incipient folklorists and anthropologists sought to be rigorously scientific, the impetus for the study of folk cultures was often at least partially the feeling that the industrial world had become disconnected from an essential, rooted, past. This sentiment, like the nationalistic impulse, meant that the affective dimension of culture tended to keep a foothold in all but the most scientific of folklore forays.

Unfortunately for Hardy, his observations and portrayals of country life, while endowing country folk with more agency than most artists, also deromanticized the folk. His novels took on the very real struggles they (along with city folk) had with modernity and with "vestigial practices" from earlier stages of human evolution. One of these, in Hardy's later novels, was marriage, which he found problematic. In Victorian England, this scientific conclusion caused a good bit of hostility toward Hardy, and after *Jude*, the novel in which his attitudes are most clearly evident, he felt his critics' attacks strongly enough that he went back to writing almost exclusively poetry and drama. (In literary circles, Hardy's last novel, s entered the canon as an important transitional novel into the twentieth century.)

It was one thing to draw on the works of E. B. Tylor (1924), James Frazer (1951), and E. S. Hartland (1904) to find survivals of barbarianism in the peasants, but Clodd and Hardy alluded to continuing practices of the people of Christian England, like church sacraments and the institution of marriage, as survivals also. When Clodd claimed that the "high mission" of folklore was "to deliver those who, being children of superstition are therefore the prisoners of fear," he wasn't referring only to Tasmanians or Bushmen but to his English compatriots as well (Kissane 1962: 237).

It is unclear whether Hardy or his contemporaries realized that his contribution had more depth and breadth than that of other collectors who did not provide the contexts that he offered. He attempts a holistic picture of a way of life that in later times might rather be written as ethnography, drawing in his works, as folklorists still do, on both aesthetic impulses and folklore as science. Working between folklore, anthropology, archeology, and literature, Hardy painted an affecting picture of a small community and included a social critique of rural life that has resonated with multiple audiences across time and space.

In many ways, Hardy exemplifies the state of British folklore studies in the last half of the nineteenth century. Hardy was an amateur. He had personal links with scholars across the disciplines who shared his interests in one way or another. He was suspicious of mainstream religion and interested in alternatives. And, he addressed topics censored by the Victorian Mrs. Grundy and paid for it.

Closeness to his rural topic made it difficult for him to refrain from noticing the impossibility of creating absolute dichotomies between primitive and modern, between provincial and cosmopolitan that others missed. His individual characters, including some women, are more analytical regarding their personal and group situations and the changes taking place around them than many folklore collectors might have imagined "the folk" to be. What to other scholars of the time might have seemed communal survivals were significant in Hardy's Wessex. But Hardy didn't portray an idealized folk community or rural folk without agency. Though his protagonists, like Hardy himself, are buffeted by the winds of change, Hardy anticipates various more recent approaches to ethnographic studies in his recognition that creativity frequently comes from the "periphery."

We risk "colonization" of the past if we ignore the subtle insights of earlier thinkers; rather than portraying a "singing dancing throng" of country bumpkins, Hardy conveyed the agency and creativity of those rural folk.

It is to be hoped that we would learn more about the field as we enter into conversations with students of folklore past and present and build up a bank of insights and data, but it's tricky to refer to this as an evolution. Some of the oldest field techniques and insights recur in later times seeming very fresh and refreshing. Hardy's work in Wessex is reminiscent of experiments going on in the latest ethnographic writing. The story of folkloristics, and of the other disciplines, too, is not one of progressing from ignorance to enlightenment.

MANNERS AND CUSTOMS

Scholars who amassed ethnographic material outside Western Europe in the vast Empire of the nineteenth and early twentieth centuries referred to their data about the colonized as "manners and customs" rather than "popular antiquities." Although they operated in different and often nonintersecting spheres from those of the scholars of local, rural, popular antiquities, they, too, in general, assumed a social evolution that resembled biological evolution and "knew" they were at the top of that evolutionary ladder.

Practices of people in Africa or the Americas labeled "primitive" or "savage," like those of the European peasantry, were thought not to have yet evolved to the level of cultivated Western European practices. According to some theories, non-Europeans were biologically "other" than Europeans and consequently were evolving differently.

DEVOLUTION VERSUS EVOLUTION

In order to account for the lore of ancient great civilizations, now weakened or colonized, survivals of "outworn cultures" (Burne 1911)—devolution—also had to be theorized. The manners and customs of living descendants of the ancients of Biblical lands, of the Greeks and Romans, or of the great Indian or Chinese civilizations were believed to contain interesting survivals of their former greatness—practices found in their everyday lives, such as folktales devolved (simplified) from ancient mythology. French scholars eagerly looked among the Berbers in North Africa for traces of early Roman or Greek influences on them. Anthropological studies and folklore collecting abroad in the nineteenth century were frequently conducted by the Western European establishment under the auspices of military officers who needed linguists and spies, of Empire builders, or of representatives of geographical societies more interested in filling in gaps on global maps and collecting specimens of flora and fauna than in the lives and languages of "savages."

In fact, the Anthropological Institute and Ethnological Institute in London, emerging from a struggle with the powerful Royal Geographical Society, relegated manners and customs to a subcategory of "biology," which was itself a subset of geography. Many, like John Hanning Speke, a fellow explorer and later an enemy of the famous explorer, polyglot, and student of manners and customs, Richard F. Burton, disdained the study of manners and customs in the course of exploring "new" lands. Speke dismissed African languages, including

Arabic, as not worth learning and as for manners, he added, Africans and Arabs "haven't any."

Although collectors of popular antiquities at home and collectors of manners and customs abroad did not necessarily cross intellectual paths, some individuals brought the two realms and many of the incipient disciplines together in their work. Lady Gregory, the Irish nationalist, also traveled widely and supported the Egyptian quest for freedom from British domination in the early 1900s. She, and Sir Richard, among others, were concerned with issues at home and abroad; with science, literature, and folklore; with nationalism(s); and with languages.

In 1863, Burton, intrepid traveler to Mecca and seeker of the origins of the Nile River, sometime president of the anthropologicals, and a member of the ethnologicals, anthropologicals and the Royal Geographical Society, writes from West Africa, where he is British Consul, to his friend and fellow mischief-maker, writer and aristocrat, Richard Monckton Milnes, that he has just published a book containing some West African myths. "I should like however to hear what you think of them and won't forget the Spider stories—see, I bribe you!" These stories are doubtless the famous Anansi stories from West Africa—Anansi being the mythological African trickster spider, and perhaps the ancestor of the Aunt Nancy trickster tales of African American slave culture.

In this case, Burton made connections between his collections of West African oral mythology, probably obtained from missionaries or African guides, and Milnes' literary, "armchair" interest in myth back in Victorian England. (Burton, too, fell gleefully afoul of Mrs. Grundy with his translation of *1001 Nights,* which had to be published privately due to censorship laws.)

Burton's life and work are usefully iconic of many of the "beginnings" or "begetting" of folklore during the Victorian age as folklorists have ranged further afield in their research venues. Burton was a folk figure himself—his sayings passed around and collected by British folk, much as the sayings of Alan Dundes became part of the lore of folklorists in the late twentieth century. For example, Burton is supposed to have been asked by a medical doctor who knew of his military service and his subsequent explorations in Arabia and Africa, "I say Burton, how does it feel to kill a man?" "Quite jolly, doctor," Burton replied, "How does it feel to you?"

Of course, Burton had his folk groups too, including his fellow students of languages (especially Arabic), fellow explorers, fellow aficionados of erotica and poetry, and fellow government employees and military men. For example, an issue among British students of Arabic was that the British government didn't realize that Arabs did not necessarily speak, read, or write their classical language but rather their local vernacular languages.

His friend Chas Clark writes to Burton on October 19, 1883, regarding life in Cairo, "All of the officers have to study 'classical Arabic.' Some try it on the *Fellahs* [Egyptian farmers] & then 'it's fun' & generally ends by the *Fellah*'s eyes getting d—d for not 'knowing Arabic,' & the *Fellah* looking and wondering 'what new language has been got up for their benefit' by the English." The frustration is palpable in Clark's letter, and sadly, this error and the frustration continues today with soldiers sent to Iraq still equipped with classical, rather than Iraqi, Arabic.

Lady Gregory, in addition to Irish nationalist causes, was also engaged with global issues. She knew socially, in addition to Max Müller and Egyptian nationalists, many politicians, writers, and scholars of the time. She introduced the poet Yeats to folklore studies and took him on field trips near her home in Ireland. She herself, like Yeats, was involved in the Irish theater and published widely on Irish folklore and on political issues. In her memoires she writes of her fieldwork, but she also tells personal-experience narratives drawn from her membership in her own folk communities, with their "gay talk and pleasant acquaintanceship and gossip that I have called folklore" (Gregory 1976: 205), an early example wherein we are all the folk.

As previously mentioned, this book is not intended to be a triumphalist story of how folklorists "evolved." Lady Gregory's views on folklore, for example, seem to have been broad enough to suit a much more recent parameter. Even earlier, in 1893, Joseph Jacobs wrote, "we are the Folk as well as the rustic, though their lore might be other than ours, as ours will be different from that of those that follow us (237).

Although the editors of the *Journal of American Folklore* of the time continued well into the twentieth century to concentrate on what they saw as vanishing folklore in America, such as "Lore of Negroes in the Southern States of the Union" or "Lore of the Indian Tribes of North America," or the "rustic," clearly Dundes' recognition that we are all the folk was in fact assumed by at least some of the earliest collectors.

CONCLUSION

This chapter touched on the environment in which folklore studies as we know them today in North America were first nurtured, especially by the British, and traced developments that have influenced the course we are now on. Many topics of interest, debate, and contention today worked their way into the conversation two hundred or more years ago, including how the discipline is involved with social justice issues, positive and negative; how and where folklore studies are done; and how folklore relates to other disciplines, many of which were launched during the same time period.

In the following chapter we look from a higher level of abstraction to generalize about how key concepts introduced here continue to resonate with other disciplines.

Chapter Two

Modern or Postmodern
The Devil Is in the Details

We are all, I suspect, a little Victorian, Modern and Postmodern at once.
— Ihab Hassan, *The Postmodern Turn*

Scholars across the disciplines disagree about when modernity "began" and when it became (if it *has* become) postmodernity. For our purposes, we will approach modernity as having stretched from the last half of the eighteenth century through the Victorian Age to the end of World War I. This time period is one version of what is often referred to as "the long nineteenth century," encompassing the swath of time when the disciplines—sciences, social sciences, arts, and humanities— as we know them today were born. During this period in Western civilization—and only Western—as Max Weber indicated, cultural phenomena "appeared which (as we like to think) lie in a line of development having *universal* significance and value" (1966: 13). This was a hegemonic claim that effectively "silenced" most of the world's voices at home and abroad in the age of Empire building.

Late modernity, as it proceeded after World War I, encompasses the beginnings of the breakdown of colonialism and the emergence of different forms of nationalism and professionalism. At the same time, the voices of folklorists and many others in the social science and humanities disciplines became louder in their questioning of social and global hierarchies. The end of the 1960s may be thought of as marking the beginning of a postmodern age by bringing to the forefront a range of measures: rethinking gender dynamics within many disciplines; resisting fiercely defended disciplinary boundaries and methodologies; challenging the canon and taken-for-granted dichotomies (such as fact and fiction, tradition and change); and revising the common assumption that scientific disciplines are always reliably objective.

To oversimplify, modernity categorizes and hierarchizes, whereas postmodernity breaks down barriers and categories—disciplines, classes, folk/popular/high culture distinctions, races, sexual orientations, and ethnicities. These are consciously subverted (though often we may be finding another place to "repackage" exclusivity). In addition, postmodernity looks for competing narratives and meta-narratives about "the" past as well as the tendency of the past and the future to collude. This breaking or blurring of boundaries, and the challenge made to "grand narratives," was happening all along, of course, but was not, and still is not today in many arenas, part of institutional narratives.

Furthermore, both the modern *and* the postmodern revolve around the wish to "clear oneself a space" (Appiah 1991: 346) either by insisting on personal, artistic, acknowledgement or by insisting that scholars stay within their disciplines (or by both) and that all nonscholars, as defined by university gatekeepers, must keep out, as Francis Utley intimates below (1953: 195). Kwame Anthony Appiah persuasively argues, "modernity has turned every element of the real into a sign, and the sign reads 'for sale'" (1991:344). He cautions, however, that "any reflexive rejection of the commodity form . . . often reinstates the hoary humanist opposition between the 'authentic' and the 'commercial'" (1991: 338 fn2). For an example, Appiah cites Kobena Mercer's work on ways "by which marginalized groups have manipulated commodified artifacts in culturally novel and expressive ways" (1991: 355). In this regard, while postmodernity has blurred reified categories we might ask if postmodern discourse has not also set up, almost inevitably, new loci of exclusivity and hierarchy.

POSTCOLONIAL:POSTMODERN::
COLONIAL:MODERN?

Appiah asks if the "post" in postmodern is the "post" in postcolonial. He answers himself that it is true that when postmodern meets postcolonial in a place like Africa or Pakistan, the predicament of the postcolonial intellectual—"a category instituted in black Africa by colonialism—is simply that as intellectuals, we are always at risk of becoming 'otherness machines,' with the manufacture of alterity as our principal role" (1992: 157). "Otherness machines" is a term taken from Sara Suleri's *Meatless Days* (1989: 105), and Homi Bhabha writes in the same vein in *The Location of Culture* (1994) that postcolonial perspectives are those "that intervene in discourses of modernity that attempt to give a hegemonic 'normality' to the uneven development and the differential, often disadvantaged, histories of nations, races, communities, peoples" (1994: 171). Putting modernity and postmodernity into conversation leads to Bhabha's observation that the postmodern mentality perceives that what he calls a "contramodernity" was already afoot in the eighteenth and nineteenth centuries, again troubling distinctions between modernity and postmodernity, discouraging the impulse to "colonize" the past.

Some ethnographers, government officials, traders, and missionaries of the colonial era were already displaced from the "party line," as it were. As such, they were colluding with the colonized, or challenging class or gender barriers, to destabilize ideas of hierarchy and category, if only out of necessity. Often this social betwixt and between-ness could occur more easily away from "home," where connections were formed across lines of race and religion as well.

Travelers often did not find a way to talk about these congenial interactions to audiences back home without being judged as having "gone native" and thus threatening their reputations; this disconnect between home and abroad helps explain the differences we often find between travelers'/ethnographers' private correspondences with their fellow travelers and the languages they drew on in their publications for a general Western audience, their reports to their governments, or communications with professional societies. Nevertheless, back in Western Europe significant numbers also resisted colonialism. Celebrated poets, especially the romantics, kept up an anti-imperial poetic discourse from the heartland of the Empire despite the heavily hegemonic nature of modernity. (See Karen O'Brien 2002 or David Erdman 1954.)

DIS-EASES

We wonder what a "professional" may be. Apparently it is a man paid by a university budget. . . . This is "budget disease" with a vengeance. It ignores the gifted amateur, the patient private scholar, the fellow-worker in another field. The informant may be the next to go.

— Francis Lee Utley, "Three Kinds of Honesty"

In these lines, well-known mid-twentieth-century American literary folklorist Francis Lee Utley addresses recurrent issues of the modern period. Having briefly characterized the most common touchstones of modernity and postmodernity, the remainder of this chapter provides an overview of scholarly preoccupations—"dis-eases" or an uneasiness about certain unresolved issues—that folklorists have grappled with, along with scholars in related fields, for at least two hundred years.

The "symptoms" of modernity and postmodernity aside, as we proceed through the book, we will see that over those years there have been certain recurrent, productive, tensions in the field of folkloristics and related disciplines—many of which were introduced in chapter 1. Each of the following chapters will provide a historical trace for contemporary folkloristics. But first, this chapter will help you recognize some as yet unresolved issues. During this time, "disease" has been a powerful trope for discord that emerges from cultural and disciplinary contacts; it draws attention to the Darwinian biological embodiment underscoring social interactions. It is not surprising that bodily experiences such as disease and related terms such as "infection" would be drawn on as metaphors related to social experience, since human bodies constitute both the social and the biological. (At the same time, biological diseases are socialized—consider a "war" against cancer, or AIDS as a punishment for promiscuity).

This tie-in between the biological and social has been interrogated in recent decades by scholars like Michel Foucault and Giorgio Agamben in their discussions of biopower and biopolitics that take us beyond the reified categories of nation, ethnicity, and creed. The question of the interstices of biological and social, addressed by both Charles Darwin and his opponents, has remained at issue, including human beings' social and biological, metaphorical and "scientific" relationships with each other, with other animals, and with the rest of the "natural" world.

DIS-EASES OF LANGUAGE: ORIGIN QUESTS AND SURVIVALS

We have been constantly drawn . . . by the movement that turns the sun into metaphor; or attracted by that which turns philosophical metaphor towards the sun.

— Jacques Derrida, "La mythologie blanche"

As we saw in chapter 1, questions of the origins of language, of differences among language communities, and of the articulation of religious practices focused on what languages could reveal about particular communities at particular times in history. Language became central to Appiah's "space clearing," locally, globally, and politically (deciding, for example, who is higher on the social evolutionary ladder and thus justified in "committing" slavery and colonialism). Those effects continued, even if scholars of language themselves were not interested in, or actively opposed to, such uses of their work.

The term "disease of language," attributed to Max Müller, drew attention to other issues that we still grapple with today. Most folklorists today know Müller as a student of mythology, especially Sanskrit myth, who popularized "nature myth theory." He tied the language of myth to the ancients, whose early religions, he theorized, emerged from an awe of nature and thus worship of natural phenomena, especially the sun. Müller used philological tools to prove that Indo-European mythic gods, like Zeus or Apollo, personified these natural phenomena. These names could be traced back to old words for "sun" or "moon" or to spectacles like the sunset or sunrise.

By the early twentieth century this dimension of Müller's work was no longer popular, or even parodied (Littledale 1906). Yet, his remains an important voice reflecting on the origins of language and on the implications of metaphorical language. The inherent dangers of this "diseased language" he refers to as the "danger of mythology . . . whether that language refers to religious or secular interests" (1861: 358).

Both the origins of language and issues of "certain mischiefs attendant upon the uses of language" (Masuzawa 1993: 60) have continued to be central scholarly issues of interest to folklorists and others whether studying expressive culture, the relationships between orality and literacy, or the consequences of creating contrastive word pairs. The latter would include, for example, "tradition" and "modernity," as well as troubling comparisons—calling a weapon of mass destruction a "peace-maker." In this sense Müller's use of "myth" as a "diseased" metaphor is more similar to the popular use of the word as a socially embedded untruth than to what scholars of religious studies or folklore would classify as "myth."

Müller's work and Darwin's work in this area remain relevant today in multiple ways. Müller asserted, in opposition to Darwin's evolutionary theory, that "language is our Rubicon and no brute will dare cross it" (1862: 360). Yet, his and Darwin's theories of language origin are similar and still resonate with scholars invested in the study of "structures of feeling" (Williams 1977) or of expressive culture. Darwin's rebuttal to Müller's "Rubicon" argument in fact echoed Müller's hypothesis that language origin was grounded in the need of various species for emotive expression. Darwin found this expressivity in music and asserted that his theory of evolution demonstrated that connection, especially in his study of birdsong in courtship and lulling baby birds.

Similarly, Müller theorized language origins via a need for an emotive language but one that only humans were capable of producing, and this to express a worshipful passion for the beauty and power of nature. Two hundred years after the birth of Darwin, W. Tecumseh Fitch writes, "Darwin's model of language evolution, based on a 'protolanguage' more musical than linguistic, provides one of the most convincing frameworks available for understanding language evolution." We are reminded even today of the singing, dancing throng in the work of Steven Brown, who in 2000 noted that Darwin's protolanguage model, which he called "musilanguage," had to depend on a group selection process (see Fitch 2009; 2010).

Müller's father worked with the Grimm brothers, but Müller became most interested in comparative religion, basically postulating that the great myths of the (Aryan) world began because the ancient Indians needed language to worship nature, that is, to find religion. Müller described his amalgam of philological, philosophical, religious, and mythological studies as "the thread that connects the origin of thought and language with the origin of mythology and religion" (1901: vii). As a philologist, he approached the past through the phenomenon of language; as a scientist, he studied phases of language development in close association with the cultural history of which they were a part.

This quest for the study of origins intersects with the work of the Grimms and others to find the roots of their languages in the tales or poems of living ancients within the rural or wild areas of Europe. In keeping with the tendency to elevate the folk and emphasize their mythopoeic mentality, Müller postulated that they came by these root words through a process he referred to as "inflection." The myths constituted a syntactical structure that emerged "naturally and directly from the innermost spiritual urge of a people (Volk)" (qtd. in Masuzawa 1994: 24). These roots, which at first were words in themselves, became corrupted, Müller asserted, and came to serve only as word endings. The ancient Buddha, he believed, was a solar deity and so was Zeus.

Again, we learn from Fitch that "Darwin does recognize the phenomenon today called 'grammaticalization': he states that 'conjugations, declensions, &c., originally existed as distinct words, since joined together'" (qtd. in Fitch 2009). Darwin linked language origin to nature but did not attribute it to a longing to worship nature. He hypothesized that humans developed protolanguages by imitating the sounds of nature and animals. Ancient Vedic myths were Müller's means of investigating the "progress" or lack thereof of religions. Müller thought that, as Buddhism spread, it "languished," becoming corrupted and mongrelized from its original "purity." But also, borrowing from the science of paleontology, he asserted that his work was linguistic paleontology, a technique that allowed him to draw on ancient myths to reconstruct and trace the genealogy, the ancient ancestral roots, of Europeans, and with a broader sweep than the Grimms had accomplished.

This preoccupation with both biological and social methodologies that would reveal the origin and spread of humankind continues today. Embedded in this study is a tension over whether particular cultural phenomena, including myths, spread from a central source or were independently invented. In the twenty-first century scientists still care deeply about the origins not only of language but of the human species and whether it emerged from a central location or from multiple locations. Fitch (2009) points out that "Darwin's . . . model and arguments [regarding language origins] remain surprisingly relevant to contemporary debates."

PURITY AND DANGER

In chapter 1 and throughout the rest of this book, the disease of language is contrasted to the purity of language. This uneasy tension manifests itself in contradictory attitudes toward language, so that, ironically, during the romantic period when Müller was writing, aesthetic language (performative or artistic language) that would have been of interest to folklorists was considered corrupt. What was needed instead for scholarly communication was modern language ("pure," "cosmopolitan," "*dis*-passionate") as defined by a relatively small group of scholars like John Locke. As folklorists Richard Bauman and Charles Briggs point out in *Voices of Modernity* (2003), that requirement effectively eliminates most of the world's peoples from the "conversation."

Contemporary scholars continue to wrestle with issues of ("authentic") discourse in folklore, as well as in medicine, sociology, anthropology, and other fields. Folklorists emphasize figurative, especially aesthetic, language, in situ, "a semantic style of investigation" that George Stocking links back to Müller and his disease of language (1987: 294). "[Müller] continued to contemplate the possibility of pure, literal signification, free of figures . . . a primordial sign announcing its own origin, a perfect word of shadowless illumination" (Masuzawa 1993: 75).

The trickiness of language weaves through the last two centuries and interweaves still with questions of "diseased" discourse in which tropes must be interrogated across cultural domains, particularly when a word or phrase appears in a new context. Local language was perhaps better kept at arm's length to separate from scholarly studies any "impurities" cast by the cacophony and confusion of local experiences and reports. Distance discouraged personal contact or familiarity, allowing decontextualizaton and then recontexualization useful to the scholar's purposes. Müller, for example, never went to India while working on comparative philology, mythology, religion, or metaphor—all of which were highly inflected by his study of Indian myths.

Of course, as Bauman and Briggs point out, purification of certain "trope-ical" diseases can thus be achieved, but this purification leads inevitably to another kind of hybrid, although hidden and privileged.

They point to stereotypical grammar teachers, as well as linguist Noam Chomsky and columnist William Safire, as contemporary examples of language purifiers. The new hybrids might be, for Safire, "welfare mothers," a code word for race, while for neocolonialists, "nonstandard" dialects might be code for irrational, ignorant, or prospective school drop-outs headed for "dead-end service jobs" (Bauman and Briggs 2003: 7).

Anthropologist James Fernandez elaborates on the disease of language, specifically the play of tropes as a "diseased condition," one that causes trouble when moving from the abstract to the concrete or vice-versa. The study of language "dis-eases" thus provides information scholars may use to justify certain classification systems (animal and human, primitive and civilized, global and local) and at the same time to confound categories and upset assumptions.

MORE ON BUDGET *DIS*-EASE

It is a main symptom of the disease of our schools, which let the kinds of knowledge fall away from each other, and waste knowledge, and time, and people. All our training plays into this; our arts do; and our government. It is a disease of organization, it makes more waste and war.

— Muriel Rukeyser, qtd. in Utley's *Three Kinds of Honesty*

Utley's "budget disease" suggests his wariness of categories and hierarchies, including concerns about the dangers of fencing off disciplines and creating disciplinary "territories." Gradually, the self-educated person, the private scholar (the public scholar working outside the university), and the gifted amateur, as well as colleagues in related fields, become isolated. On this topic, Utley quotes the poet, activist, and feminist Muriel Rukeyser. When he wryly predicts that the informant will be next to be ejected from the club, he draws attention to another disease in which different "kinds of knowledge fall away from each other" (qtd. in Utley 1953: 196)

For Utley, though, the budget disease arises from both trying to navigate cross-cultural shoals and shutting off interactions that are necessary for good scholarly work. Drawing hierarchical lines might be called not simply the "budget disease" but the "disease of modernity." He laments the coming devaluing of the informant, at which point folklorists will be cut off from the very essence of their discipline. This lament points to the seldom achieved goal of developing methodologies that allow for collaboration with informants.

In the 1950s, Utley was already retreating from the "exclusivity of insight" that is at the core of modernity: how one must be correctly credentialed, whether by power, centrality (West versus the rest), wealth, or training; whether disciplinary or academic, amateur or "professional," and so forth. Ironically, to be able to rail effectively against this disease of "modernity," what William James (1987: 97 called "branding, licensing and degree-giving, authorizing and appointing, and in general regulating and administering by system the lives of human beings," requires a license or degree, or at least authorization by someone who has one. To be fair, however, in the United States this has been partly a move toward "meritocracy," even if it has not acceptably transcended issues of class, race, ethnicity, gender, or sexual orientation.

"SOCIAL" *DIS*-EASES: BETWIXT AND BETWEEN

I heard Mansour say to Richard, "You transmitted to us the disease of your capitalist economy. . . ." Richard said to him, "All this shows that you cannot manage to live without us. . . ." They . . . said such things to each other as they laughed, a stone's throw from the Equator, with a bottomless historical chasm separating the two of them.

— Tayeb Salih, *Season of Migration to the North*

The Sudanese writer Tayeb Salih published his novel, *Season of Migration to the North*, in Arabic in 1966 (the English translation was published in 1969), ten years after Sudan gained independence. Drawing on the disease (infection, germ) motif, Salih artfully interweaves and interrogates four loci of tension—colonialism, racism, classism (including rural vs. urban), and sexism/gender. Thus, *Season* is a useful exemplar for the following chapters as it foregrounds in all their complexities many "postmodern" and "postcolonial" anxieties also long grappled with in folkloristics and related literary and social scientific fields and in the public arena. These continue to be confounding.

Focusing on two thousand years of circum-Mediterranean encounters and orientalist complexities, it is clear for Salih that dysfunctional power relationships are collusive. In essence, the mysterious character, Mustafa Sa'eed, colonizes the "North" (Britain) by conquering both Western academia and Western women, thus inverting colonizers' othering of Africans as feminine, earthy, uncivilized, and premodern, while encouraging British women's fantasies of African exoticism in order to seduce them. "My [London] bedroom was a spring-well of sorrow, the germ of a fatal disease." (1969[1928]: 34).

And yet, Salih's nameless narrator, passively suffering diseases of hybridity, finally, on the verge of drowning in the middle of the south to north rushing Nile, chooses his betwixt and between life.

CONCLUSION

In the end, the issues that students of folklore and disciplinary fellow travelers wrestled with over two hundred years ago (or more) are still with us. Drawing in this chapter on examples from art, music, religion, language, and literature whether in periods called premodern, modern or postmodern, we see how issues of *dis*-ease with the status quo are confronted affectively, as hierarchies, categories, and dichotomies are troubled creatively. In the following chapters we will look further at the power and potential of expressive culture. As various scholars in this chapter remind us, the past is not past, a thought important to keep in mind, or we may fall back into colonizing and "purifying" it, rather than learning from it.

Chapter Three

Aesthetic Discourse and Cultural Affect

PART ONE: DEFINING LORE

In 1846, William Thoms suggested the word "folk-lore," a "good Saxon compound" to replace "popular antiquities," "bygones" and "manners and customs." His particular interest was in collecting literary (folklore in/as literature) and historical ("old customs and feelings,") items of the British bucolic rather than in social scientific studies. Thoms' choice of the word folklore engaged Britain's Saxon past while also disengaging from labels like "popular antiquities," which evoked French etymology, and from the German *Volkskunde* being used then by Wilhelm Riehl, a German scholar of folklore as a social science. As we saw in chapter 1, European nations sought to retrieve their unique, organic pasts via recovery of local verbal art believed to be from days of yore and thus representing the roots of a particular emerging nation's soul or spirit.

In various journals, including the famous literary journal the *Athenaeum*, Thoms offered examples of genres, "manners, customs, observances, superstitions, ballads, proverbs, etc., of the olden time" (1996[1846]: 863) that needed to be harvested before they disappeared. He likened folklore to a crop of corn, of which only a few ears remain to be gathered. Even today, the popular notion remains that folklore is something aesthetically compelling that is disappearing. Although most folklorists have widened their definition of lore, we continue to be drawn to folklore perceived to be disappearing and at the same time essential to a rooted future, whether as local or world heritage.

While many, like Thoms and Riehl, focused on their own local or national lore, others were comparatists, identifying and labeling similar motifs historically or geographically. How did an item of lore evolve, or, devolve (as we saw in Müller's studies)? Did similar items originate independently or were they the product of diffusion? Consider the origin and spread of particular folktales—the oldest version of Cinderella, for example, whether written or spoken—or of folk medicine—say, the formula for a particular healing potion. Efforts to trace, categorize, or classify local lore around the globe meshed well, at least superficially, with similar scientific methodologies in other disciplines, such as studies of the origins and development of language, classifications and categorizations of language families or plants and animals, or efforts to establish the origins and biological evolution of Homo sapiens.

Structures of Feeling?

> A particular sense of life, a particular community of experience hardly needing expression, through which the characteristics of our way of life . . . are in some way passed, giving them a particular and characteristic colour . . . a particular and native style . . . it is as firm as "structure" suggests, yet it operates in the most delicate and least tangible parts of our activity. In one sense this structure of feeling is the culture of a period . . . and it is in this respect that the arts of a period . . . are of major importance.
>
> — Raymond Williams, *The Long Revolution*

What is lore? As much as lore has been studied, its definition is shaky. The American Folklore Society (AFS) website lists several definitions (http://www.afsnet.org/?page=WhatIsFolklore). Raymond Williams' (1977) definition of structures of feeling delicately conjures some particular essences—"of colour," "of style," "delicate," "least tangible," "arts," "feeling." Like folklorists, Williams sought to define and understand communal affect in a society—recognizing its centrality and its capacity to enact change. Thoms also recognized the centrality of affect in his reference to "feelings." Williams' definition difficulties and ours resonate with folklorist Mary Hufford's (1991) observation that lore is often "hidden in full view."

Perhaps the truest thing about the lore of us folk is that it is recognized by a communal—"artist(s)" and "audience(s)"—fashioning of cultural aesthetics; "expressive culture" or "affecting culture," implying some artistic or stylistic attempt to "perform" (see chapter 5) with one's community. This performance encompasses, as Bauman writes, "artistic *action* . . . and artistic *event*" (1984:4). No matter why and by whom lore has been studied, scholars have recognized a communal exchange and negotiation of artfulness, creativity, and energy—depending as much on an audience that "gets it" as on a "performer." Some artistically constructed, communally engaging quality draws us to lend special attention to these nuggets, as Thoms did, and to classify them into specific genres (riddle, myth, legend, or complex communal customs like American Thanksgiving or the Jewish Seder), even though analysis of their artistic dimensions has not always been attended to, even by folklorists.

Genres

Despite the drawbacks of trying to fit aesthetic discourse and the study of cultural affect into global generic categories, attention to genre has been at the core of folkloristics, but often with more attention to the product than to the process or producer. So, for example, we have volumes of myths, folktales (tales of a Chinese or other "exotic" grandmother), legends (Robin Hood), jokes, and proverbs with little information about who told the story or the joke and to whom and under what circumstances. In fact, before this artistic "product" becomes an object of academic study or national pride, it has frequently been wrested from its folk community and fitted into one "etic" or "universal" genre or another (etic genres are discussed in more detail in the next section), cut from its moorings by folklorists, sociolinguists, cultural anthropologists, historians, or any of the myriad scholars who study narrative today.

Some definitions of folklore are simply composed of a long list of genres. In 1965, Alan Dundes provided this partial list in his essay, "What Is Folklore?":

> myths, legends, folktales, jokes, proverbs, riddles, chants, charms, blessings, curses, oaths, insults, retorts, taunts, teases, toasts, tongue-twisters, and greeting and leave-taking formulas. In addition, it includes folk costume, folk dance, folk drama (and mime), folk art, folk belief (or superstition), folk medicine, folk instrumental music (e.g., fiddle tunes), folk songs (e.g., lullabies, ballads), folk speech (e.g., slang), folk similes (e.g., blind as a bat), folk metaphors (e.g., to paint the town red), and names (e.g., nicknames and place names). Folk poetry ranges from oral epics to autograph-book verse, epitaphs, latrinalia, limericks, ball-bouncing rhymes, jump-rope rhymes, finger and toe rhymes, dandling rhymes, counting-out rhymes, and nursery rhymes. It also contains games, gestures, symbols, prayers, practical jokes, folk etymologies, food recipes, quilt and embroidery designs, house, barn and fence types, street vendor's cries, sounds used to summon animals or give them commands. Other forms are mnemonic devices (e.g., the name Roy G. Biv to remember the colors of the rainbow), envelope sealers like SWAK, and comments made about body emissions like burps or sneezes, and customs for holidays. (1965a: 3)

Defining "folklore" by providing a list of etic genres does give non-folklorists an idea of folklorists' central objects of study. However, it echoes those lonely lists of folktales, folk cures, and so on, that we find in popular collections of folklore. We find books of quilts with pages of beautiful quilt patterns, perhaps a word about their romantic(ized) history, but without consideration of the processes by which the patterns are formed or "performed." We are given little idea of the artist or artisan, no consideration of how or when a quilt was designed, or how its design was inspired or (re)negotiated by a particular community of quilters.

As we have seen, ideas about how to approach genres were drawn, consciously or not, from disciplines such as biology and geology, and from a cluster of human sciences in which folklore studies were perceived to fit, but such studies neglected concerns of individual or local creation or of "living traditions." Folklorists early on wanted to proceed "scientifically." To be taken seriously, folklore and other new disciplines needed to follow the contemporary rubrics of science. As such, George Laurence Gomme, historian and founding member with his wife, Alice, in 1878 of the British Folklore Society, wrote that folklorists, since embracing scientific methodologies, "are no longer considered harmless lunatics prettily chatting to each other about fairies, Mother Hubbard, and little Red Riding Hood" (1893:25).

As noted in chapter 1, folk genres were labeled "survivals" analogous to biologists' labeling "vestigial" our wisdom teeth or appendixes, or the leg bones of whales (that is, items useful in earlier times, but no longer). Lore, likewise, was largely thought to be on its way to extinction, of no use in the industrial world. Lore had had a purpose in the agricultural world, but, heading into the twentieth century, for better or worse, those last ears of corn would finally disappear. Other scholars, drawing from physical anthropology, equated folklore with fossils frozen in time. "Vestiges" in Freudian psychology were remains not of a primitive past but of infancy—the cause of neuroses in adults. Sometimes the two terms were used interchangeably.

For example, Captain John G. Bourke, briefly president of the American Folklore Society, concluded his 1893 article, "The Miracle Play of the Rio Grande," a folk play of the birth of Jesus produced by inhabitants of "Mexican ranches and towns" (89) in southern Texas by noting, "There are settlements of Irish, Welsh, English, Scotch, Germans, Danes, Swedes, Norwegians, Canadian French, Russians, Poles, Italians among us, and surely some of them must have preserved "vestiges" and "survivals" [of folk dramas] fully as important as [the Rio Grande miracle play]" (Bourke 1893: 95). Like many early folklorists, Bourke's fascination with the still lively communal practice stemmed partly from its documentation as having traveled from the Canary Islands without much change over the last two hundred years and also with his assumption that it will not be around much longer—hence references to "vestiges" and "survivals."

Etic vs. Emic

Etic Genres: Folkloristics as Science.   Because we take notice of
aesthetic moments we tend to label them (as "legend," "folkdance,"
"hopscotch"). In doing so, we assign them commonalities across communal groups, and that process can help us recognize similar phenomena in many cultures, although we start hegemonically from
a Western classificatory system. Etic genres are useful for providing some idea about a kind of lore we assume most cultures would
have—"riddle" or "lullaby"—and we can look for it wherever we are
in the world.

For example, I went looking for lullabies in mountainous north-
western Tunisia during the winter snows of 1969 and was told by
Maltese nuns, who ran a nursery school there, that Tunisians didn't
have lullabies. I suspected that could not be true, and, indeed, it was
not. The nuns had introduced me to a teenaged girl named "Snow"
(*Thalja* in Arabic), who took me to visit mothers who would let me
record their lullabies. Still today the well-respected folklorist Barre
Toelken explains the need for etic genres by drawing an analogy with
biology: Doctors do not talk about the body without knowing all the
principal parts. So, too, folklorists, "without a generic terminology . . .
would have little hope of understanding each other" (qtd. in Sims and
Stephens 2005: 12).

Such exercises in classification link back, of course, to the mid-
eighteenth century when new scientific disciplines were emerging.
Latin classifications of plants, animals, rocks and minerals—global
classificatory systems—were meant to bring order to "chaotic" nature,
as Mary Louise Pratt characterized them, and create a common discourse across empires and their spheres of influence. As we will see
in a later chapter, bringing order to chaotic *culture*, as it were, proved
more difficult, but anthropologists, linguists, and folklorists tried.

While some early modernists did attend to local genres, the
impetus was toward a global classificatory system such as other scientific disciplines were producing. Gomme believed that for folklore to take its place as a scientific discipline, careful classification
was needed. In 1885 he stated in "The Science of Folk-lore," that to
find its place among the sciences folklore terminology needed to be
systematized. Gomme created a classificatory system for folklore
genres with "natural" divisions among narratives, customs, superstitions and beliefs, and folk speech. One of the subcategories of
narrative was folktales, and by 1910 the Finnish folklorist Antti
Aarne published the first motif index. Tale-type and motif indices
were efforts at global classification of tales and motifs within them,
similar to classifications of genus and species in biology or global
classifications of languages.

Emic Genres. Emic genres, then, would be those generic names for lore recognized by a particular culture group. Although useful, etic genre labels can cause us to miss ways that artful moments are distinct and to overlook the significance of differences across communities. Today, the tendency of folklorists is to study the folklore of communities "on their own terms"—from an emic perspective. Rather than using etic designations, folklorists in the field seek names for genres particular to the folk group they are learning from. They then use these emic genre terms in addition to or instead of an etic term when sharing their field research.

Such an approach allows the folklorist/ethnographer to develop more complex understanding of how a particular genre works in relation to other elements of expressive culture within a community. This approach also helps the folklorist (1) take into account genres that are important to the group, but are not identified in the "global" schema, and (2) be sensitive to the fact that while a genre, the lullaby, for example, may seem similar across cultures or groups, it may in fact be different in form or content, or in how it is drawn on in social interactions. Such differences are blurred by the use of one (etic) term for all vaguely similar folk art forms. Moreover, discovering new ways of engaging with expressive culture may help folklorists reperceive aesthetic habits of their own folk groups.

In etic studies, similarities are foregrounded, whereas in emic studies differences among communities are emphasized. "Lullabies" as found in particular global locals can be quite different from what we might assume from our own experiences in terms of performance venues, range of possible texts or melodies, texture—perhaps in anything but the intent to sing a child to sleep. Thematic content, for example, might differ considerably. Bess Lomax Hawes, in "Folksongs and Functions: Thoughts on the American Lullaby" (1974), theorized that only we Americans distance our children from ourselves in our common lullabies. In one, a baby is in a tree (and the poor thing falls out!); in another, the baby sails off in a boat. Hawes thinks such distancing might be caused by our expectation (a dominant American folk idea) that our children should leave home—go off and be independent.

Context may also reflect cultural expectations for an independent life, starting with the unusual North American custom of putting the baby in a separate room to sleep. Babies are spatially isolated both literally and through the words of lullabies. Other contexts can also be different—singing in a quiet place, for example, or in the midst of a lively gathering. Rhythm (texture) varies in lullabies of different communities, as well. Ewe people in West Africa rely on a complex, syncopated rhythm, Hawes reports, rather than the simple 4/4 or 3/4 time of the typical American lullaby. Such differences in text, texture, and context are deeply embedded "folk ideas," as Dundes (1972) calls them, and are common to a particular cultural worldview. In the case of lullabies, different locals not only model different communicative styles but imagine different futures for their children.

(Against) Genres

> *A... political rally, for example, is a secondary genre comprising some combination of the primary genres of speeches, songs, dress, slogans, and dances.*
>
> — Lisa Gilman, "Genre, Agency, and Meaning in the Analysis of Complex Performances"

> *At best, then, the term "legend" is probably a term of convenience which should not be taken too literally; at worst, it may be a misleading simplification.*
>
> — Gillian Bennett, "Contemporary Legend"

The trouble with genres is that when they are reified (concretized), they stultify dynamic processes. Patrick Mullen argues, for example, that "as a genre of folklore, belief is an impossibly unwieldy construction" (1996: 119). Even if it weren't, genres (whether etic or emic) have other problems. In relegating artistic culture to genres, we risk neglecting the flow among various loci of lore, the sum of which is drawn on by folk to perform and negotiate a folk community. The lack of attention to multiple contexts of any folk moment is also what critics of folklore point to when they argue that folklorists are too romantic, finding shelter in studies of folk productions and avoiding the grim realities of life. But expressive culture does grapple with those grim realities and so do the folklorists who study it.

Here are some examples of "impossibly unwieldy" genres that folklorists have addressed. Folklorists like Henry Glassie (1982) and Ray Cashman (2008) focus at length on an Irish folklore genre called a *céilí* (evening socializing among neighbors), and in Egypt the folklorist Dwight Reynolds (1995) considers a similar genre, the *sahra*. These both resemble occasions in the La Have Islands that Richard Bauman describes simply as evening sessions of male sociability at the general store (1983: 340–41)

While Bauman's and Reynolds' examples involve only men, women in Kelibia, Tunisia, also hold time-of-day defined get-togethers, which sometimes, like the *céilis*, include men and women and all ages, from babies to elders, enjoying in afternoons or evenings refreshments and lively conversation (Webber 1991). "At-homes," coffee klatches, and salons are similar Western, class-oriented events. Among college students in the U.S. the genre might be closest to what is known as "hanging out," as in asking, "Do you want to hang out tonight?" or just showing up at a neighborhood bar, café, or *sheesha* lounge where friends are likely to be found.

As far as I know, this sort of folk practice, a space for socializing defined by expected times of day, participants, and venues, does not have an etic genre classification. There are differences among these practices in various locals, but, in general the genre is marked by impromptu get-togethers, occasions for nuggets of performance to emerge in a semiprivate folk community setting. Those might include reminiscences, impromptu storytelling, joking, creative cussing, and music making, often within the context of other activities that are not folk activities per se, but have a folklore dimension, like card games or chess. Sometimes, but not always, the events are gender specific. These "occasions" are akin to mini, everyday, spontaneous "festivals," moments of communal relaxation outside daily work routines. The genre is also probably less open to being captured by commercialization than other smaller gatherings like birthday parties or Thanksgiving.

Another genre that does not have a formal name in the etic realm is group strolling, what Giovanna Del Negro and Harris Berger refer to as "ritual promenade" and what in central Italy is called *passeggiata*. Perhaps the Easter Parade on New York's Fifth Avenue or the focus on costume while strolling at the Kentucky Derby are somewhat similar, although those events happen only once a year and the *passeggiata* is a weekly event that involves people-watching, but not with the formalized intensity of the watching at the Easter parade or Derby.

In Columbus, Ohio, a monthly event, the "Gallery Hop," stretches from afternoon into late night on High Street's liminal arts district between The Ohio State University and downtown. Most small establishments, whatever their everyday businesses (restaurants, hair salons, boutiques, an ice cream parlor, art galleries, a fair trade shop, and so on) stay open late for the event. Most feature an artist, often local, for the event. Suburbanites meet city folk, youth meets age, town encounters gown, and alternative, folk, and institutional art genres (visual, musical, foodways, and dance) intermingle. As in the *passeggiata*, people watch and are watched, crowds meander in and out of the shops, and streams of slow-moving cars cruise the street, sharing it with strollers, dancers, and street musicians who overflow the sidewalks.

These strolling genres are interesting to folklorists because they resist global classification, as well as for at least two other reasons. First, they are an occasion to study expressive culture sign systems (semiotics) that incorporate all five senses, a sensual experience that might culminate for some even in art inscribed on the body—a tattoo from a local parlor or henna art. Second, the art itself is just one visual dimension; others include the visual presentation of self by strollers; the architecture; the festively gussied up street, with displays of flowers, banners, and decorated shops; and so on. Study of these events illustrates the problem with genres as building blocks for folklore scholarship. Genre-based studies tend to ignore process and concentrate on product, amputating the flow of expressive culture across media and among various rhetorical and artistic resources.

Scholars in other disciplines draw on folk genres in their research but tend not to focus on their affective power and their centrality to communal synergy. For the folklorist, this misses the point. A fine social anthropologist of Asian studies from my graduate days at Berkeley, Wolfram Eberhardt (see Eberhard and Nailî Boratav 1953), valued folklore and published widely in the field. He put together a Turkish tale-type index while marooned in Turkey during World War II and, some years earlier, a Chinese tale-type index, and published collections of Chinese and Turkish folktales. Yet, these were kept separate from his studies of culture, and he once remarked that folklore was what one collected in the field while relaxing after the hard work of the day was finished (his own *sahra*, I suppose).

Similarly, anthropologists may insert a collection of riddles or stories at the end of a text or in a separate publication. Linguistic anthropologists and discourse analysts tend to unpack the *structures* of utterances in minute detail, whereas folklorists most often privilege unpacking *expressivity*. To folklorists, expressive culture is the central focus of attention in their work. Why? If one is trying to understand a particular folk group (and both "understand" and "folk" have had different meanings over the last two centuries), then attention to lore in its creative contexts allows insight into core cultural complexities. Once a community member takes the time to craft folk music, verbal art, a garden, a pot, or a cure, the folklorist knows that the item has an aesthetic logic that needs attending to as condensed culture—part of a complex communal "conversation."

In a folk genre, just as with other institutional art forms—an Auden poem or an Arbus photograph—we look for what the performer of the genre might be saying about the past and the present, and what the future of the community might be. An interesting distinction between folk and institutional genres (high or popular culture) is that folk genres require more communal negotiation. A community is interlaced with neighborhood or hometown people of various walks of life and does not generally comprise only other storytellers, artists, writers, or craftspeople but their knowledgeable audiences and critics as well. At the heart of attention to genre is attention to expressive culture, to shared sentiments. To look for new genres, we look for where folk put creative energy. Folklorist Nick Spitzer once told me that when he worked at the National Endowment for the Arts in the 1970s, the NEA had a slogan, "Support the arts, that's where the people are." Spitzer said that those working in the Folk Arts division changed their slogan to, "Support the people, that's where the art is." Rather than bring opera to the Eskimos, see what music the Eskimos have to offer.

Folk Genre Hierarchies?

Some folklorists have preferred to create a hierarchy of genres based on dubious distinctions of "purity" or "antiquity." For example, coal miners' lore, like that of urban populations, was often rejected by folklore scholars. Apparently the purity of the productions of denizens of the land did not extend to those coal encrusted men at work beneath it, or to lore that felt new to folklorists. One senses that this lore was a little too raw for ballad scholars whose corpus of material also focused on inequities, disaster, and grief, but in contexts romantically set off from ongoing grim realities.

John Spargo, like many folklorists of his day, was a social reformer who seems to have felt that ballads weren't for miners, calling their ballads "quasi-literacy" (1944). In a response to Spargo's remarks, Benjamin Botkin, wrote: "It is time that folksong scholars stopped thinking of folksong in terms of the English and Scottish ballads. It is time that they did a little more digging in the rock. Then they might understand what the miner sings about when he says: 'And while he was working For those that he loved, The boulder that crush'd him, It came from above'" (1944: 139). Here, a direct rebuttal to the favoring of "old" lore.

Tradition and/Is Change

The instability, multilayeredness, and slippery qualities of aesthetic discourse (or cultural affect) allow it to be a potent resource for negotiating personal and communal shakeups through manipulation of "text," texture, or context. *Romancing the Real* (Webber 1991) demonstrates that change is as much a part of tradition as is stasis. Shared communal stories, jokes, or other compressed nuggets of culture can be managed to persuade one's communal in-crowd to accept or resist changes in communal norms as well as creative adjustments to the lore itself—various dimensions of its, perhaps multiple, "text(s)," texture(s), or context(s), or the medium in which it is performed.

The structure and content of a folk art genre or event can remain unaltered, but changing circumstances and discourses for which it is deployed—the context—can reframe the way in which the energy of the genre is directed. Family stories take on new, or intensified, meanings when the family is meeting a fiancée for the first time. On a larger scale, every dimension of the Mardi Gras festival in New Orleans was imbued with a message of resistance ("We are still here, bloody but unbowed") after Hurricane Katrina, a display of festive normalcy after that ruinous storm. The holiday of Ashoura is, for Shi'a Muslims, a day of mourning for the martyrdom of Husayn, grandson of the Prophet. For some of my Iranian refugee college students after the 1979 revolution and turmoil, Ashura became a personal day to display grief over forced separations from family and country—even for those who were not particularly religious.

So text, texture, and context are all available to be imbued with the immediate needs of a community. Or those ingredients of customary lore may be altered. A story reduced to a proverb takes on a life of its own. In a small North African town, during World War II, a townsman, Gacem l'Englese, was cheated by Italian occupiers out of the price of his homemade butter. He tells a story about his revenge, selling the occupiers clay pots filled with mud with a thin layer of butter on top. When Gacem first told the story after the war, his friend responded, "If one pot had fallen [breaking open], Gacem would be dead." *Tah hallab, meyyit Gacem* [a fallen pot, Gacem's dead] is now a proverb in the town. Some know the original story and some do not. More than half a century after the incident, story and proverb survive—one chronicling a particular series of events and the other generalizable to any time one survives audacious behavior.

The power of a recognizable genre can frame vastly different kinds of cultural content (cf., Gregory Bateson [1972] and Erving Goffman [1974]). Proverbs a community shares can encourage members to see a situation differently, and proverbs carry the weight of communal wisdom. If my mother-in-law and I start criticizing someone, she often stops herself to say, "We can't really judge her unless we walk a mile in her shoes." The common folk saying, "Before criticizing a man, walk a mile in his shoes," might echo the point of a folktale, be found in a song, or be changed, so that the speaker might say, "Walk a mile in my shoes," thus claiming his critics have neglected the old folk saying that should be invoked on his behalf. (It's a joke, too: Walk a mile in someone's shoes before you criticize him—you will be a mile away and you will have his shoes.)

Conclusion

Part One focused on settings in which verbal lore is central and provided a loose definition of what identifies the lore folklorists study. Borrowing British scholar Raymond Williams' term "structures of feeling," I try to give readers a "feel" for the loosely structured aesthetic creations that folklorists study—centripetal forces that hold a community together despite stresses of poverty, war, or natural disaster. In Part Two we turn to the development of what is now an integral part of folklore, material culture.

PART TWO: MATERIAL CULTURE

In short, [folklore] covers everything which makes part of the mental equipment of the folk as distinguished from their technical skill. It is not the form of the plough which excites the attention of the folklorist, but the rites practised by the ploughman when putting it into the soil.

— Charlotte Burne, *The Handbook of Folklore*

What Charlotte Burne, first woman president of the British Folklore Society, referred to a hundred years ago as "technical skill," what today is "material culture" (visual presentation of self, from dress to tattoos; food-ways; house types; boats; or musical instruments) even in Dundes' list of folklore genres compiled some fifty years ago is overpowered by verbal art genres. Marginalization of material culture studies perhaps derived from early folklorists' strong ties to the literary. Further, the artful and communal processes of fashioning such materials, whether of a plough, a carpet, a boat, or a quilt, were rarely part of their study. Due to the pref-erence for old artifacts, the creators of the artifacts were often long gone.

Yet, in the late nineteenth and early twentieth centuries, the study of such "technology," "old technical processes," or "plastic arts"—"material culture"—hovered just outside folklore's door in Britain and North America peripheral to "the mental equipment of the folk." A glance at the *Bibliography of Folklore, 1905* and the *Bibliography of Anthropology and Folk-Lore, 1908* name similar artifacts to those asso-ciated with material culture today from agricultural tools (including "the plough"), architectural styles, weapons, barbering implements, and musical instruments to boats, dolls, graves, toys, "footballs," and baskets, beads, combs, cooking utensils, lace, looms, and pottery. Sometimes scholars of folklore studied these material items and even published on them, though not often under the rubric of folklore.

North American, unlike British, folklorists of the late nineteenth and early twentieth centuries did not exclude the study of "the mate-rial objects of culture," but in both North America and Britain, most folklorists homed in on verbal art, ritual, festival, and music. Who, then, *was* studying material culture a hundred years ago, and how did its study (re)emerge as an integral element of folklore studies?

The story is complicated by the fact that at that time many schol-ars, unbound, worked among disciplines and with/as public intel-lectuals. While material culture was largely the province of artists, anthropologists, geographers, historians, or archeologists, these scholars often moved in the same sphere as folklorists. Sometimes they were, in addition to their other métiers, folklorists themselves. C Marius Barbeau was one such. A prolific early-twentieth-century Canadian ethnographer, he was on the board of the *JAF* and also served as an early president of AFS in addition to affiliating with well-known anthropologists like Franz Boas and linguists like Edward Sapir, as well as working closely with noted geographers and historians of his day. Although Barbeau published on the origins and diffusion of textiles, vernacular architecture, and, most notably, totems, in addition to French Canadian and Native American songs, myths, and tales, almost none of his material culture (as opposed to ballad or myth) studies appeared in folklore journals despite his close identification with the discipline. Boas, although he considered folklore a subset of anthropology, did not publish his studies of masks, totems, or other Native American material culture in the *JAF*, but often did in the journal *Science*.

Awkwardly and artificially, it seems to us now, objects of material culture that are ingredients in the creation of moments of heightened communal expressivity were separated disciplinarily from their place alongside dance, music, song, and verbal artistry, as if, in describing the Mardi Gras in New Orleans, analyses of music and dance could be divorced from foodways, costumes, and floats. Despite such awkward divisions, during the late nineteenth and early twentieth centuries, some artists and anthropologists made significant contributions to material culture study that resonate within the realm of folklore today.

Early Material Culture Studies

Here are two examples—one of North American scholars studying Native American material and another of German ethnographers researching material from German New Guinea. Both research projects were underwritten by their respective governments and by private enterprise, each in its own way colonialist, and each manifesting an impulse to salvage ways of life thought soon to be lost. Acquiring items of material culture, as we will see, often had tragic consequences for indigenous people.

Interest in material culture of Native Americans or Pacific Islanders might center on the communal (rarely individual) aesthetics of fashioning, say, a basket, mask, or pot, or might revolve around what study of construction techniques or trading patterns could reveal about historical relationships within a culture group or with nearby groups. Anxieties at that time among field researchers about the authenticity and purity of lore was manifested in their efforts to prove that the art or craft had long been practiced.

Scholars wanted to show that material examples were "pure," not influenced by whatever scientists considered civilization. Materials produced before contact from the West were "best." U.S. artist and museum preparator William C. Orchard, in his 1916 monograph on porcupine quill decoration among Native Americans, cites the mention of such decorations by "early explorers." Orchard notes, "It is reasonable to suppose that porcupine-quill work is an art whose practice antedates the advent of people from the Old World and their influences on the arts of the American aborigines" (1916: 3). As was typical, Orchard considered older artifacts to be of better quality.

North American Artistry. In contrast to its many publications on Native American verbal art or religion, the JAF was not then a publishing venue for material culture, and Orchard's research on the fashioning of Native American housing, cradle boards, baskets, hair brushes, and beadwork was seldom referenced in articles therein. Although an artist and museum preparator, his work was ethnographically informed. The intermingling of disciplinary approaches—of anthropologist, artisan, and artist—shed a brilliant light on process, on the high levels of artistic skill and technical savvy needed to fashion Native American folk arts and crafts.

His interest extended to visits to Sioux reservations in the Dakotas and to the Ojibwa in Ontario, where he was taught the production of quill decoration from porcupine trapping, to preparing dyes, to the methods and patterns used in the finished products. He was sensitive to the social lives of Native American artisans and to their (emic) measurements of good workmanship. Further, making "familiar" what might be considered "strange" practices, Orchard equated embroidery with quill work and observed that both expect the underside of a piece to look as "finished" as the top. Finally, in an interesting intervention into diffusion studies and presentation of self, he pointed out that Indians who were most skilled at quill work were not those among whom quills were plentiful. He wrote: "This may indicate that our Indian friends, like white people, desired the things most difficult to obtain for their personal adornment" (Orchard 1916: 3).

Orchard, like Barbeau with his totem studies, clearly chafed under the assumption of quality differences between folk and "fine" art as well as the elevation of artists over artisans. Perhaps because they had practical uses—butter churn, quilt, stone work—or perhaps because of their ephemerality, or their status as the work of women, minorities, or working-class men, crafts were aesthetically less valued than "art." Orchard, however, considered beadwork and quill work fine art despite decorating practical products such as hunting materials, belts, or containers and despite, or perhaps because of, their use of natural materials. He underscored their complex designs, the tireless patience needed to produce them, and the "inventive genius" of the designers.

Diffusion was another concept that claimed Orchard's attention, doubtless through his association with cultural anthropologists, especially Boas, although Boas studied diffusion of languages, verbal arts, and religious practices rather than the diffusion of material culture. Orchard noted the complexity of measuring the diffusion of material artifacts since the value laid on rarities meant that artifacts or their components might not be from neighboring communities but acquired through hard travel to distant lands over difficult terrain, as in the case of porcupine quills or the dyes used on them. Even in the diffusion of tales, palaces often pop up in stories not where palaces are plentiful, but precisely where they are not.

Another scholar who dedicated himself to Native American studies at the same time as Orchard is Boas' student Frank G. Speck. Anthropologist and folklorist, like Boas, he also once served as president of the AFS. Yet, despite his many publications in the *JAF*, his material culture studies appeared elsewhere. There are perhaps four reasons for this trend: First, although folklorists did publish in the *JAF* on American Indian verbal art and religious practices, arguably Indians would have been considered the province of anthropologists (students of the "primitive") rather than of folklorists (students of the nearby rural).

Second, by the end of the nineteenth century North America had numerous governmental and academic organizations that incorporated study of Indian material culture under the umbrella of the histories and cultures of American Indians. These studies are models, in their origination in political expediency, for today's area studies (Middle East, Latin American, African, or Asian). Third, as discussed above, although many folklorists did find the study of Native Americans within their purview, they didn't see material culture as folklore, exactly. Finally, in the mind of Orchard, quill works merited evaluation in the context of high art. This leads me to speculate that the pesky categories of folk, popular, and high art, in addition to those of disciplines, led folklorists to set aside consideration of material culture until the last third of the twentieth century.

People of "Nature," People of "Culture." Meanwhile in Europe, folklorists' attention to material culture continued n under the rubric of folk life studies—but set apart from the verbal arts. Boas' former teacher, the German scholar Adolf Bastian (1826–1905) traveled widely but was especially interested in the Pacific Islanders colonized by Germany—barely a nation itself (1871). Described as a Renaissance man, Bastian studied law, biology, and finally medicine, but along the way he developed a passion for ethnology—comparative ethnography.

Like so many others of his time, he wanted to be scientific but was dedicated to recovering disappearing "natural" cultures. Studying these, he thought, would lead to understanding universal elementary ideas shared by all humans—a point of view that later influenced structuralists (see chapter 6).

Bastian believed that "people of nature" were important for understanding elementary ideas because they were closer to them than "people of culture" were. Both Bastian and his former student, Boas, searched for the spirit or *geist* of a community, although Boas favored language and verbal art study in his search for particular examples of universal essence, while Bastian thought material culture was more reliable. Bastian identified regional spheres of influence through the study of material culture circulation (diffusion) rather than the circulation of myths, tales, or rituals. He organized material culture displays in German museums to identify the relations among culture groups.

By the nineteenth century, the material culture of non-Western, "exotic," or "primitive" peoples had been categorized and hierarchized by Westerners in three overlapping ways: culturally, aesthetically, and commercially. To put Bastian's work in context, by the 1600s the Spanish had already shown interest in artifacts, *particularidades* (or curiosities) of the Pacific Islands, but they dropped their interest when the artifacts were found not to be marketable. Artifacts brought back from distant lands, termed "oddities," "rarities," or "curiosities" were also displayed in European or U.S. drawing room cabinets without cultural context. It was only when scientists in the nineteenth century hierarchized and categorized them in a global context as *ethnographica* that they took on widely the value of art pieces—of course "value" was judged by European standards whether "scientific" or aesthetic.

As Appiah neatly sums up, once modernism in the form of universal classification and scientific standards was in place, "primitive art was to be judged by putatively *universal* aesthetic criteria, and by these standards it was finally found possible to value it" (1991: 12). The name of the producer, conveniently for the collector, did not matter. Perhaps more than any other kind of lore or plant, animal, or even human "specimens" brought back to display for profit or to propagate for medicine or food, artifacts were immediately and forcefully commodified and wrangled over—again, the emphasis was on the communal and not the individual. Missionaries and commercial agents were most likely to be at the collecting forefront, spending time in places that Westerners considered attractively primitive. Some collectors wanted merely to be recognized by scientific societies for their contributions, but others cared little for the scholarly enterprise and were intent on plunder, making handsome gains by loading up on "natural" (flora and fauna) and human-made (material culture) prizes to sell off.

This resulted in scrambles for artifacts, which, at best, had laughable consequences and, at worst, tragic ones for indigenous people. Bastian in 1874 had a Prussian navy ship bring back artifacts from New Ireland and New Britain, both Pacific Islands Bastian perceived as untainted by Europe, still pristine, and frozen in time. The race was on to get navies, traders, missionaries, and so on to acquire artifacts. Although Bastian and his colleagues linked artifact collection to the goal of understanding regional indigenous mentalities, early colonial administrators treated the artifacts themselves as "national treasures" and colonial resources (Buschmann 2009: 71). Although the goal of Bastian and his colleagues and successors was to imbue their collected artifacts with ethnographic context, often the simplest contextual details were lacking—past owner(s), uses, and so on. One collector reported buying all his artifacts while drinking with a white trader who was later so hung over he couldn't recover enough before the collector's ship sailed to relate any information concerning the artifacts' provenances.

Tensions mounted among collectors. Traders and commercial agents highly valued masks and other artifacts used in religious rituals, while some missionaries wanted them burned, as they considered them to be idolatrous. Unlike Bastian, who opposed colonial annexation despite profiting from it, many settlers on native lands were "invested" in maintaining the idea of the cultural inferiority, and thus exploitability, of natives. It was counterintuitive then, in their eyes, to appreciate Islanders' artwork as "high" art, unlike Orchard's appreciation of Native American quill work. Settlers in the Pacific needed to "primitivize" items of material culture in order to justify land acquisition and forced labor. Thus, a common German term for Pacific Islands artifacts was "firewood." Some struck a balance between representing material culture as both "primitive" and marketable. Nicholas Thomas reports that in Fiji, settlers referred to certain artifacts as "cannibal forks," emphasizing the "savage" nature of indigenous people (1991: 165–67). One might pay for such a fork, but part of its value was the retention of the perceived exotic, perhaps fearsome, otherness of the maker.

Bastian worried that Westerners, by their very presence, were ruining the "fragile social fabric" of native folk, but at the same time he and other ethnographers in their haste to salvage the material culture of "people of nature" engaged the very agencies (commercial agents, traders, missionaries, military) that he implicitly condemned for causing the demise of the "natural" Island cultures he had been hoping to learn from (Buschmann 2009: 20). This was literally true in some cases, for as European traders arrived they infected the vulnerable indigenous inhabitants with deadly malaria, so that one small island, Wuvulu, lost 40 percent of its population.

While colonial settlers wanted material culture for profit or decoration, ethnographers "repurposed" it as ethnographica—for Western scientific inclinations and for profit. Thus, people who lived on two German-colonized Pacific Islands, Wuvulu and Aua, understood that their artifacts were valuable to Westerners, so they fashioned more to sell to them. By the turn of the twentieth century, Islanders were bartering their artifacts for German items, and ethnographers then began to distinguish between artifacts that were "polluted" (manufactured more quickly using Western tools or artificial dyes) and "authentic," no matter if they fulfilled the same ritualistic purposes.

When ethnographica were no longer available, Europeans began plundering grave sites for attractive artifacts. Shortly after Bastian's death, his fears of ruining the social fabric of the Islands were realized with "the lethal confluence of commercial and ethnographic interest" in the region (Buschmann 2009: 126). In the end, Bastian's efforts to organize curiosities scientifically as "the key to understanding themselves" through "a comprehensive exploration of humanity at large" (Penny 2003: 88), gave way in the early 1900s to the reorganization of museums to tell popularized, nationalistic stories using material culture to "rank" global cultures as less-to-more evolved. Even before that, however, the goal of museums to attach indigenous meaning to material culture items supplied by trained anthropologists was seldom met. Bastian was a victim of his own "success." In Berlin in 1886, he opened the first free-standing museum of ethnographica, which was intended to offer a "complete comparison" of the world's material culture. Fifteen years later it was so crammed with artifacts that it was less a museum than a global jumble (Penny 2003: 86–87) and a fire hazard. Until after the First World War, many German anthropologists continued to consider material culture "the central text of their discipline" (Buschmann 2009: 104), but movement toward less global, less material, and more in-depth, local studies had begun.

Material Culture and Folkloristics

As late as the 1950s Sona Rosa Burstein, in her presidential address to the British Folklore Society on the science of folklore, still excluded material culture study from folkloristics. "I should unhesitatingly fail [a candidate for a diploma in folklore] who included material objects in the definition; but I should with equal briskness fail a candidate who could not make a good showing of answers to a set of questions on the material accessories of folk-life and lore!" (1957: 334). Although Burstein acknowledged that in Germany and Scandinavia material culture was considered folklore, she ranked material culture as a "cognate study" along with anthropology, history, archeology, and language. For Burstein, material culture items were simply accessories to folklore. And the situation in North America

wasn't much different. By the end of the First World War, diffusion-
ist studies drawing on material culture were growing apace in North
America. In the 1930s, geographer Fred Kniffen became known as a
specialist in folk architecture, was warmly welcomed into the society
of folklorists in the late 1940s, even serving on the AFS Council for
three years 1951–1953 and publishing at least four articles on material culture in folklore journals during that time period. But, by 1959,
he had resigned, disappointed that few in AFS shared his interest "in
the material manifestations of folkways, such things as are of concern
in the folk museums of Scandinavia" (qtd. in Vlach 1995: 330). Almost
immediately thereafter, in 1960, folklorist Warren Roberts, whose
early work was on ballads, returned to Indiana University after a
year researching Scandinavian folklife in Norway, to introduce folklore courses on material culture, shifting his own research focus to
tree stump tombstones and log buildings in Indiana.

Over the next twenty years, one student of Fred Kniffen, Henry
Glassie, brought folklorists' concern with *expressive* culture to the
attention of students of material culture who had been focused
primarily on technique or diffusion. This focus on the affective
dimension of material culture benefited from folklorists' attention
to semiotics, a field of textual/textural study that did not privilege
literary theory but emphasized attention to sign systems across multiple media and genres. Glassie's publication of *Passing the Time at
Ballymenone* (1982) demonstrated the enrichment to folklore studies of interweaving multiple genres and media, including those of
material culture, and at the same time drew attention to individual
artists and artisans.

One final note: In 2006 a project started at the Pitt Rivers
Museum, Oxford University, and called "England: The Other Within"
identified artifacts in the museum that were part of the English collections—not necessarily objects obtained in England, but those collected
by the English. This project has now (re)placed tangible material culture items alongside intangibles that folklorists had concentrated on
in the past—offering a fresh look at how "Englishness" is constructed.
The researcher, Allison Petsch, writes on England: The Other Within's
home page that "those folklorists who are identified as being part of
Dorson's 'Great Team' or were very prominent in the Folk-Lore Society
did not donate to the Pitt Rivers Museum, whilst those people . . . who
were 'footsoldiers' in the Society were more likely to give significant
collections. In addition it is interesting to note how often their dona-
tions mirrored their folkloric interests." Here again, we find folks from
multiple disciplines, as well as nonacademics, gathering around a project focused on reintegrating lore, tangible and intangible, into myriad
contexts, both immediate and global.

CONCLUSION

The focus on structuralism and semiotics in the latter part of the twentieth century opened up a discourse in which the study of sign systems was less dominated by literary or verbal art genres. At the same time, performance studies overcame the limitations of a focus on genres and took a more sweeping regard for context and process as well as product. A reversion in the age of postmodernity to more permeable boundaries among disciplines and between university and public scholars, as well as the fracture of rigid barriers marking off the imaginary (reified) categories of folk, popular, and high art, were phenomena that made room for new insights into how folklore, and certainly material culture, might be more productively studied.

Chapter Four

The Folk Soul vs. the Primitive Mind

In short, in dealing with Folk-lore, much was said of the Lore, almost nothing was said of the Folk.

— Joseph Jacobs, "The Folk"

As the disciplines developed in the nineteenth century, "primitives" (or "savages") meant roughly "folk," (or "peasants") that were living in less developed, less "civilized" (in the eyes of the West) parts of the world. "Popular antiquities," and later, "lore," were the folklorists' equivalent of primitive "manners and customs" when found among the rural folk of the industrialized world. For a long time in folklore studies, whether armchair or ethnographic, we saw and heard very little of the folk, "peasants" or the so-called primitives or savages, as unique individuals or thought *full* communities. Ignoring, dismissing, romanticizing or in a variety of ways "othering" the producers of the lore allowed its manipulation to serve the elite as "powerful ideological weapons in debates about political direction, cultural values and national identity" (Martin 1993 qtd. in Trubshaw 2002: 6) not necessarily at all in conformity with the intents of individuals or folk groups from which they were "plucked," or "gleaned."

FOLK AND FOLKLORIST

Thoms' 1846 equation of lore to nature's bounty, ears of corn to be gathered from the field, accords the creative role of any particular individual about the same notice as a particular corn stalk. In fact, the Grimm brothers had used the same "lore as corn" analogy in 1812, and in America, by 1888, William Wells Newell, writing in the first volume of the *Journal of American Folk-lore*, alludes to American colonialists as a new hive of bees, swarmed from the old world. These extended metaphors underscore perceptions of the folk (or "primitive" or "peasant") as nature's children, bound close to the soil. The editor of *Athenaeum*, John Collins Francis, in seconding Thoms' proposal that readers send in lore examples understands lore to be "old customs and feelings,"—unreflective, emotive, crude—and this is often the closest we get to assumptions about the actual purveyors of the lore.

The shadowy term, "feelings," evokes a general understanding at the time of what most thought folk to be good for. They represented a way to preserve elemental sensitivities and intuitions thought to be disappearing under industrialization and urbanization. (Sometimes, but not always, as we have seen, this recovery of the soul of a people could be the grounding on which to build a nation.) In the mid-nineteenth century, these *folk*—the keepers of a "civilized" people's *geist*—were the amorphous peasantry in rural areas peripheral to the advance of civilization untouched by the impurities of urban life. The "primitive" or "savages" were found in unexplored or newly "discovered" lands, at least until American folklorists started including Native Americans as primitives on their own shores. In both settings, social change was the culprit. According to Anatoly Liberman (2008), "Railways were the main bugaboo of those who watched the rural landscape disappear under the wheels of the devil, the steam engine. Being run over by a train became a literary motif." Elsewhere change was marked by the coming the white travelers or settlers, or earlier, the intermingling of what were perceived to have been once pure cultures, ethnicities, languages, or even tribes. After these events, lore was considered more problematic.

All of this underscores the relative importance, from the perspective of most early folklorists, of the owners of the lore versus the lore itself or its gatherers. As a community, peasants bore the folk soul of the people, embodied the emotional base of a nation, according to Herder. But for the most part, their traits were presented in glittering generalities—one farmer a prototype for all farmers, one fair young maiden much like another, crones interchangeable. Further, folk were not generally thought to be able themselves to articulate the rooted values found in their own lore—they needed "civilized" intermediaries.

Jack Zipes, in his book on the Grimm brothers, reports that the brothers sent a circular asking their correspondents to act as intermediaries and to find people of a certain class—miners, shepherds, and fishermen, but also children and old women—from whom to gather lore. Their names were rarely known, and their songs and stories often altered, a practice many folklorists themselves defended as simply part of the folk tradition. For example, we typically know the names of some purveyors of lore to the Grimms, rather than the names of people whose tales the brothers wanted. Many of these intermediaries were educated, middle- and upper-class (young) women repeating stories of nannies or grandmothers or even stories read in books. In important ways, as we will see, folklore scholars today continue to struggle with the relationships between the folk as studied and folklorists as studiers and the ethical dilemmas that relationship engenders.

As discussed in chapter 1, the folk not only were considered anonymous in the late-nineteenth and early-twentieth centuries but were typically represented as creating lore communally. James Frazer (1951) in his famous *The Golden Bough*, the twelve volumes of which appeared between 1890 and 1915, represented human actors as cogs (a king or a farmer) in a folk community, participating in "barbarous" cults, rites, and myths. Frazer found that the folk, under the domination of fearsome and glorious nature, enacted similar myths globally. In each case they performed rituals related to the sacrificial killing of god-kings to ensure bountiful harvests. Frazer theorized that for millennia, folk from cultures around the world had encountered similar problems and enacted similar solutions. Not all agreed, however. In a speech to folklorists in Britain in 1893, folklorist Joseph Jacobs remarked that communal creation was a "fraud, a delusion, a myth." In these remarks, he draws on a folk saying followed by a proverb to support his thesis,

> Let us try to realise in imagination what must have happened when, for the first time, the saying was uttered that was afterwards to become a proverb, or a tale that was destined to be a folk- or fairy-tale, was first told. Was it the Folk that said the one or told the other? Did the collective Folk assembled in folk-moot [folk meeting] simultaneously shout, "When the wine's in, the wit's out," . . . ? No, it was some bucolic wit, already the chartered libertine of his social circle, who first raised hearty guffaws by those homely pieces of wisdom. The proverbial description of a proverb, "The wisdom of many, the wit of one", recognizes that truth. (1893: 234)

Critical thinking skills do not belong only to the literate and are not learned only in the classroom. Such witticisms, like other lore, could be built on, negotiated, or contested by others in the group.

Nevertheless, folklorists, anthropologists, poets, and artists were inspired by their own communal vision of the "people of nature" as preserving for the "civilized" access to the mystical, emotional connection between the physical and the spiritual, the communal soul or spirit. Another influential armchair scholar at the turn of the nineteenth century was the Frenchman Lucien Lévy-Bruhl, who in the first decade of the twentieth century postulated a divide between the Western mind and the primitive mind published a work entitled, *The "Soul" of the Primitive* (1966[1927]). Lévy-Bruhl, like Max Müller, was interested in how religion manifested itself among the primitive, who were associated with preliterate communities, whose members he described as having "archaic mentalities"—again, closer to nature, communal and mystical.

So, while folklorists and others elevated communal lore as a response to the harshness of the industrializing world, they often did not notice its individual creators who were relegated to the lower classes or "othered" as members of global communities considered lower on the evolutionary ladder. Colonialists and believers in manifest destiny (American expansionism or moral exceptionalism) justified their domination of others, especially people of color, on the basis of what they took for granted as the colonizers' superior rationality. Like the Grimms' intermediaries, much of Frazer's data were obtained from queries he sent to administrators throughout the British Empire as well as to missionaries around the globe.

By the late 1800s, more folklorists and anthropologists, perhaps due to increasingly in-depth local ethnography, were becoming skeptical of the theory postulating two kinds of human minds: one emotional and communal, the other rational and individual. Franz Boas published two articles in the *Journal of American Folk-lore* early in the twentieth century (1901 and 1904) in which he concluded that differences between the "primitive mind" and the "civilized mind" are cultural rather than "fundamental differences in mental organization," but that is not to say that the primitive or folk mind was not still, in Boas' thinking, at a lower evolutionary stage of development.

The idea of studying the primitive mind remained part of Boas' studies of Native Americans (1894, 1901). We civilized, he noted, appreciate the primitive mind but must use our reasoning powers and repress our emotional life. Nevertheless, he mentioned Western artists, musicians, and religious leaders as examples of "civilized" people who need not repress their emotional lives. These categories of the "civilized" can retrieve for us from the folk community the values of the emotional life. Here, as in Wordsworth's *Ode* (discussed in chapter 1) we see those intimations of the "primal sympathy" that remain in spite of the transition to the "philosophic mind." Still, these early informants tended not to have names or individual voices even while they provided aesthetic, religious, or national inspiration.

FEAR OF GOING NATIVE

Blowing continually into the hollowed-out body of a dead animal while fingering pipes that replace the animals' legs may have driven these fieldworkers sufficiently out of their minds to get past their alienation and the peculiarly Western problem of music as noun or object.

— Christopher Small, "Whose Music Do We Teach Anyway?"

In chapter 2 we considered certain tensions in the relationship between observer and observed—the felt need to maintain a voice of scholarly authority while evading charges of elitism. "Fear of going native" is a condition describing the efforts of colonialists, explorers, anthropologists, and folklorists to avoid becoming (or being judged by colleagues as having become) too much like the "other"—the "primitive" or folk among whom they spent significant amounts of time. Richard Burton was widely accused of having "gone native" during his time in the military in India due to his attraction to the affective dimensions of other cultures, whether sensual, religious, or social.

The more time he and other Westerners spent among the "other," the more they seemed to look over their shoulders to demonstrate to those back home they were still "civilized." In folklore circles even today, traces remain of a similar felt need to distinguish oneself from the "other" folk as scholarly participant observers while fulfilling the delicate task of representing a folk community on its own terms. Ethnographers' or proto-ethnographers' reportage for a very long time was expected to be laboratory-like—"disembodied," "sense-less" (Fabian 2000: xiii). Ethnographers downplayed relationships with intermediaries: The roles of homegrown helpers like guides, translators, porters, drivers, lovers, friends, and others who enable entrée into otherwise inaccessible communities are often erased or underrated even more than are subjects of study—especially when the investigator returns to more familiar ground linguistically, socially, and academically.

Cultural anthropologist Johannes Fabian argues that European explorers in Africa between 1874 and 1909, often feverish, ill, and overly self-medicated with alcohol or drugs, were forced into close negotiations with Africans. Africa is a continent that Europeans defined as "empty" before they began to explore it in the eighteenth century. Elite Europeans sought "scientific" control, not appreciation of native arts and emotions. Fabian (2003: 3) writes:

> European travelers [his 'proto-ethnographers'] seldom met their hosts in a state we would expect of scientific explorers. . . . More often than not, they too were "out of their minds" with extreme fatigue, fear, delusions of grandeur, and feelings ranging from anger to contempt. Much of the time they were in the thralls of "fever" and other tropical diseases, under the influence of alcohol or opiates . . . , high doses of quinine, arsenic, and other ingredients from the expedition's medicine chest.

While seeking to be scientific, they drew back from "the world as we experience it with our senses" (Fabian 2000: xii)—"sense-," thus producing senseless studies. Folkloristics is one answer to that missing element—cultural affect—in ethnographic studies, along with a turn of attention not to the virtuosity of ethnographers but to deferring to that of informants.

Although some of these expeditions evinced an interest in local languages, more often languages were described as debased and inferior, and justified for many a lack of interest in verbal arts. Jerome Becker, Fabian reports, larded his writings with Swahili words but wrote of Swahili speakers getting by on three- or four-hundred words, implying a poverty of language that "reflected reduced communicative capacities or needs on the part of its speakers" (qtd. in Fabian 2000: 2). Why would explorers resist speaking or respecting the language of the local Africans they encountered? By not speaking African languages, the explorers established an illusion of superiority and control. That all-knowing illusion was crucial to maintain, since in the field of nineteenth century Africa, they were dependent on many others (African, Indian, Arab, Portuguese) as well as things (weapons, weather, their very minds and bodies, all unreliable).

Fabian notes that explorers saw Africans as theatrical yet tended not to study performances, moments of compressed culture, but rather to be nettled by them as counterproductive to the scientific mission. Still, as Fabian notes, imperialism was itself a theatrical enterprise staged back home in the form of scholarly and public exhibitions, lectures, books, and articles. He notes a few instances of a "breakthrough into [appreciation of] performance," what he calls, "a striking instance of ethnography that comes from an act of surrender to the experience" (Fabian 2000: 120). Fabian quotes Becker writing in 1887 about a soundscape he encountered in Zanzibar:

> What kind of mysterious work is going on in the secrecy of a private home, playing a carillon that fills with muted vibrations this new island of sound from one end to the other? Quite simple—it is the act of pounding coffee in cast-iron mortars. Of lifting the pestle in time and striking the metal wall. The muffled sound, crushing the beans that first had been roasted in large basins, represents the useful; the vibration that is added, the pleasant. And this combination transforms a rather insipid chore into an intimate concert. (qtd. in Fabian 2000: 120)

Why could Becker appreciate this particular performance? Perhaps it was because in that moment he did not have to interact with Central African women in any way at all.

By the early twentieth century, making a space for oneself (see Appiah 1991) had become a question of possessing academic credentials. During Robert Lowie's 1916 final presidential address to the American Folklore Society, he continued to "deny utterly that primitive man is endowed with historical sense or perspective: the picture he is able to give of events is like the picture of the European war as it is mirrored in the mind of an illiterate peasant reduced solely to his direct observations." This from a folklorist!

Although folklorists and others now privilege such direct observations and the wisdom behind them, Lowie was anxious to separate scientifically trained scholars from peasants and primitives: "As we cannot substitute folk-etymology for philology, so we cannot substitute primitive tradition for scientific history. Our historical problems can be solved only by the objective methods of comparative ethnology, archaeology, linguistics, and physical anthropology" (Lowie 1917: 167). Lowie found, to his surprise, that many in the American Folklore Society were alarmed by his perspective, and this tension echoed that of many scholars when categories are so reified. But, as mentioned in chapter 2, it's still hard to escape this privileging of the insights of "cosmopolitan" us even by post-modern us.

Appiah gives an example from 1987 that also privileges "cosmopolitan" us. For a show at the Center for African Art in New York, nine of ten cocurators were asked to look at photographs and pick ten pieces for the exhibit. One cocurator wasn't allowed to pick because he was only familiar with the art of his own people and "African informants will criticize sculptures from other ethnic groups in terms of their own traditional criteria." Ironically, David Rockefeller, a cocurator who was allowed to choose and who, as Appiah writes with gentle sarcasm, would never "criticize sculptures from other ethnic groups in terms of their own traditional criteria" chooses one sculpture because, "I thought it was quite beautiful . . . the total composition has a very contemporary, very Western look to it. It's the kind of thing, I think, that goes very well with . . . contemporary Western things." He chose another because, "I own it," and others because of their market value, conflating aesthetics with the marketplace (all quotations are from Appiah 1991: 337–38).

As scholars studied the lore of folk closer to them geographically and in terms of class, and as more folklore scholars immersed themselves in "exotic" places, distinctions between scholars and other folk became more difficult to maintain, as communities became better at talking back. In 1957, Sona Burstein, in her remarks as president of the British Folklore Society, noted that anthropologists were finding "anthropological investigations here at home, among their fellow-citizens, are rewarding in results" (338). She added, "A little while ago a member of this Society asked me, 'What about the folklore above stairs?'" (338). "Above stairs" is code for the privileged classes, "downstairs" for servants. By 1970, when Richard Dorson wrote, "Is There a Folk in the City?" most folklorists were comfortable both with folk in the city and folk in the suburbs.

OF PURITY, AUTHENTICITY,
AND LEVELS OF FOLKNESS

Nevertheless, as we have seen, we tend to see hierarchies of folkness or of lore, a kind of continuum based on what seems, to use a dangerous measure, "more authentic." This desire for authenticity, however imagined, was and still often is shared by artists and folklorists studying expressive culture. Recall that William Orchard thought older Native American quill work done before the advent of the Europeans was superior—authentic, pure, and so on.

In John Spargo's 1944 review of George Korson's *Coal Dust on the Fiddle*, miners and their ballads are unabashedly compared to ballads and ballad makers of British origin: "To some it will seem noteworthy that miners should write ballads at all; but after reading a few of these carelessly-written verses, some readers will take an attitude like the one Dr. Johnson expressed about a dog's ability to walk on its hind legs" (91). Spargo is referring to Samuel Johnson's famous eighteenth-century comparison of a dog walking on its hind legs to a woman preaching: "It is not done well; but you are surprised to find it done at all." I submit that Spargo rejected miners' lore as inferior to old British ballads that scholars continued to seek among Appalachian mountain folk at least partially because the miners' lore was not seen as old, pure, and authentic but rather as too closely connected to the "unromantic," messy lives of the performers.

Spargo's not unusual attitude explicitly ranked communities in terms of their members' abilities to perform. Of course this ranking depended not on a community's assessment of its own lore, in this case folk music, but rather on folklorists' expectations, which were in turn based on an evaluative scale derived, like Rockefeller's, from experiences with preferred and oftentimes their own communities. In a 1944 reply to the review, folklorist Ben Botkin lashes out at this insult to miners' music and recalls the assertion of Joseph Jacobs, writing, "in our study of folklore we should pay attention not alone to the Lore, but also to the 'Folk,' especially the 'Folk of to-day.' It is hard to believe that fifty years after this [Jacobs'] statement we find a reviewer in the pages of this JOURNAL writing about the coal miners of the United States as if they were performing animals" (Botkin 1944: 139). Botkin urges more time in the field, remarking that there is dust on the fiddles of folklorists, smelling not of collieries, but of the library. Similarly, Bob Trubshaw writes a well-wrought critique of scholar Cecil Sharp's negative influence on British ballads (Trubshaw 2002: 151–152; but see as well C. J. Bearman's [2002] passionate defense of Sharp).

At the same time, folklorists could be impatient with other disciplines' disrespect of folk creativity and intelligence. We find in 1894 Boas (who classified folklore as a subfield of anthropology) vigorously critiquing in his vice-presidential address before the American Association for the Advancement of Science the belittling of the creativity and organizational skills not only of Native American communities but of individual Indians known to him. Having rejected Herbert Spencer's (the famous biologist and social evolutionist) assertion concerning Natives' impulsiveness, with the repost that they show "great foresight," Boas goes on to critique Sproat's (presumably Scottish-Canadian entrepreneur, officeholder and author, Gilbert Malcom) ascription of lack of concentration to his First Nations informants asserting that often he would be "the one who was wearied out first.". Rather "the traveller" tends to ask "trifling" questions in a foreign language.

Furthermore, Boas asserts that particular Native Americans are indeed creative, citing examples of changes in myths and beliefs made by individual tribal sages whether by borrowing or through inspiration—exactly the same as that of the "civilized philosopher." Nevertheless, Boas and others are stingy with life stories or even names of those who possess these idiosyncratic talents, something later folklorists and anthropologists would come to regret (all quotations are from Anonymous 1894: 251).

AT HOME AND ABROAD:
TRAVELERS, MISSIONARIES,
ANTHROPOLOGISTS, AND FOLKLORISTS

It is now almost impossible, for example, to remember a time when people were not talking about a crisis in representation. And the more the crisis is analyzed and discussed, the earlier its origins seem to be.

—Edward Said, "Representing the Colonized"

An important struggle within disciplines emerging over the last two centuries is the struggle over who speaks for whom. White upper-class men decided that physical characteristics (color of skin, shape of head, characteristics of sexual organs) signaled intelligence, integrity, and "good breeding." Not surprisingly, after measuring and categorizing many global populations, those privileged white men found that they had the physical signs that proved they were highly evolved. In fact, as we now know, they fudged the numbers. As long as researchers did not feel a need to communicate with the "object of study," they could assume that most human subjects had nothing to contribute.

But the particular dilemma for ethnographers studying expressive culture was that their discipline expected them to speak the language of their informants. Early examples of informant agency came when the ethnographer sat at the feet of the Other as apprentice in an art form both enjoyed. Thus, the little book on falconry in Sindh written by Burton in 1852, reveals respect for Sindh customs and for his friend and mentor Meer Ibrahim Khan. Burton asserts that he vastly prefers the fellowship of Sindh falconers to being cooped up with the company found in an English breakfast room or at Oxford.

Similarly, early studies of music leveled the cross-cultural playing field as the researcher or Western musician became the student, at least in the language of music. Yet, it would be Westerners who would most profit from these musical encounters. By the second half of the twentieth century musicians and folklorists more often acknowledged their folk music teachers. Roger Abrahams' edited volume *A Singer and Her Songs: Almeda Riddles' Book of Ballads* was published in 1970. The Rolling Stones' Brian Jones, and others, studied and recorded with the Joujouka musicians in Morocco in the 1960s, and folklorist Dwight Reynolds in the 1980s apprenticed himself to a rebab player when he was studying poet-musicians in Egypt. In all cases, their debts to particular musicians are acknowledged, interest in the musicians' lives is evident and sustained, and the context for their repertoires is elaborated.

TALKING BACK

Although early accounts of the lore of the folk "other," denied agency to the individual artists and often to entire races or ethnicities, sometimes those same folk found ways to talk back. In 1902, African American W. E. B. Du Bois published *The Souls of Black Folk*, each chapter beginning with a musical notation from a spiritual. Du Bois claimed these songs exist "not simply as the sole American music, but as the most beautiful expression of human experience born this side the seas" (Du Bois 1904: 251) Though trained in history and sociology, not folklore, Du Bois interwove a lyrical prose text with carefully chosen examples of black spirituals, displaying through them an often politically powerful aesthetic.

Du Bois as well underscores the felt national need for a communal "signature" aesthetic for the United States, reminiscent of myths, legends, or other nationally rooted expressive culture of European folk. From spirituals came jazz, often claimed, in its seduction across race, class, creed, and ethnicity, as America's only true art form. Thus, "black folk" and their expressive culture forms are de-exoticized and placed at the heart of what it means to be American.

We have long been used to critiques of urban, often white, musicians or scholars of folk songs who gather up from rural and black musicians folk songs that they then use to make their own reputations. From early on, some rural musicians were aware of this appropriation for profit. Howard Odum, a sociologist, collected songs of southern African Americans over the first decade of the twentieth century, concentrating on the repertoires of individual "songsters," a term black performers then preferred over more generically limiting labels such as "bluesman."

Odum's informants were aware that Odum reached a wider audience to whom their work should be acknowledged. Odum said the singers he studied sometimes could substantiate claims of authorship and that some singers attempted to protect their songs and those of others from the collector. One young man Odum recorded called out his name before each song he sang into the graphophone (an early recording device), "Song composed by Will Smith of Chattanooga, Tennessee." Occasionally he would hesitate and sometimes give the name of another as author. Other times he just announced, "sung by Will Smith" (Odum1911a: 256).

Despite Smith's attempt to control his and his community's talent, Odum showed little interest in him or the story surrounding his musical life, although Odum was not compelled to seek out origins considering original in some sense every performance even of a single performer in a new context. When informants had aspirations to be their own authors, this continued to create tension within the scholarly hierarchy, whether scholars were working in their own backyards or farther afield. But informants often resort(ed) to speaking around or in the margins of the work of ethnographers.

BETWIXT AND BETWEEN: A CONFUSION
OF CATEGORIES

The great and fundamental fact [is] that all legends are the gradual result of combination from many sources by many minds in many generations.

— J. N. B. Hewitt, *Iroquoian Cosmology*

A college education is in most cases a valuable training . . . to do excellent and original work in scientific research, but in the others it becomes a leaden cowl, making its wearer a narrow-minded bigot and pedant fully knowing the full sum of human and divine knowledge.

— J. N. B. Hewitt (qtd. in *Histories of Anthropology Annual*)

*The College insists too much on established authority and is often apt
to generate a feeling of caste, . . . both of which tendencies are incom-
patible with human progress in the attainment of truth and justice. . . .*
                                        — J. N. B. Hewitt (qtd. in *Histories of Anthropology Annual*)

In this section we will look in some detail at individuals who
found themselves betwixt and between in the imagined folk/scholar
great divide, as they work with the expressive culture of folklorists. It
seems useful to take an in-depth look at a few personalities to see how
various people resist classification and have helped make the divisions
Utley laments more permeable, enriching our understanding of the
power and possibilities of folkloristics. Of course, there are many ways
to find oneself betwixt and between. In the examples below, we see
not people who "went native" but people who "were native"—or were
they? Each found his or her own means of confounding expectations
and making a space for him- or herself, each more or less successfully.

John Napoleon Brinton Hewitt

Hewitt was someone who had the advantages, but also the dis-
advantages, of having been considered by the scholarly folk community as "betwixt and between," both in his heritage and in his lack of
university credentials; at the time, both heritage and, increasingly,
a university education were marks of distinction. The first quotation
above is chosen from Brinton's work with the Iroquois cosmology, a
nice representation of his ideas of folk collaboration on legend formation over time. The second two are taken from replies he wrote to a
young Native American girl who wondered if she could achieve scholarly credentials without going to college. Anticipating by fifty years
Utley's 1953 comments cited in chapter 2, Hewitt's replies reveal a
good bit about his own situation and his own frustrations.

Hewitt's father, an orphan adopted by and raised as a Tuscarora
Indian who became a doctor, drew on both Anglo and Native American medical knowledge in his practice; his mother was half Tuscarora.
Hewitt was an anomaly in two ways to conventional scholars of the
time. Was he Native or Anglo? Was he a scholar, an informant, or something else—a go-between? His Native identity gave him a distinct edge
in data collection and interpretation. He was mentored by the great
Chief John A. Gibson and spoke Iroquois languages, but his dual ethnicity also made him "other," both personally and in scholarly circles.

I suggest that conventional scholars were uncomfortable with the
confusion of categories wherein a person could perform as both Native
American and Anglo American, informant and scholar. We find echoes
of this discomfort with Hewitt even decades later. William Fenton, a
folklorist of Native Americans who met Hewitt in his last years, took

a dig in a 1962 article at this "other" who dressed "inappropriately," either to his heritage or his station. "He had married again late in life," Fenton writes, "and his wife, who claimed dowager rights in old Washington society, had gotten him up to look like a Smithsonian scientist: wing collar, Oxford gray coat, striped trousers, and white piping to his vest" (1962: 287). Perhaps he saw Hewitt as going "un" native.

Maybe not surprisingly, Hewitt's transition off the Tuscarora reservation came through an encounter with another sort of "other," a Jersey City society woman, Erminnie Smith. Smith had borne four sons and taken them to Europe to be educated simultaneously while further educating herself. She acquired German and French and trained in geology. Upon returning home in 1876 at age forty, she joined the American Association for the Advancement of Science (AAAS), where she met John Wesley Powell, also a geologist, who had recently turned to ethnology and organized the Bureau of Ethnology. She became interested in anthropology and started the Aesthetic Society for Women, which had an inventive combination of interests in science, art, literature, and the domestic arts (home beautification and hospitality, for example).

Although a woman, Smith's social status and family connections, in addition to her European education, allowed her to associate with men in the scientific world. Powell offered her the support she needed to do research into the folklore and languages of the Iroquois, and on a trip back to her hometown of Marcellus, New York, she was introduced to Hewitt. She hired him as her assistant, and they collected folktales and mythology, as well as studied the languages of the Tuscarora and other Iroquois. It was Smith, however, under the sponsorship of Powell, who presented their findings to AAAS, and in 1885 she was elected secretary of the anthropology section of AAAS. She and Hewitt continued to work together over the next six years, though Hewitt had to take other jobs as well. Midway through 1886 Smith died suddenly at barely 50 years old, while she and Hewitt were working on a Tuscarora-English dictionary. Hewitt, at his request, was hired to finish it.

By the last two decades of the 1800s, when academic credentials were beginning to be important for scholarly credibility, Hewitt began to run afoul of new, formally educated scholars like the folklorist and anthropologist Daniel A. Brinton, who had studied both at Yale and in Europe. Brinton was an advocate of scientific racism (not unusual at the time) and a rival of Hewitt's employer, Powell, whose experience was all in the field. Powell was interested in analyzing the data he had acquired during fieldwork. Largely self-taught in natural history, he also placed very little value on formal education, hiring people with proven ability rather than degrees.

Brinton, although he did no fieldwork, also considered himself an expert on Native American languages. Widely read, he put his trust in European linguists, who tended to support the assertions of earlier students of Indian languages about the languages' chaotic constructions. At the time, Brinton's academic credentials trumped Hewitt's Indian and fieldwork credentials in the scholarly community. Brinton wrote that Hewitt's comments on Indian language structure were flawed because Hewitt, he intimated in a rather vicious review of Hewitt's work, could not read the German scholars.

While other fieldworkers on Indian folklore and language defended Hewitt, Brinton's scholarly credentials were such that his library work was given more credence than work in the field. Elisabeth Tooker and Barbara Graymont write that, "few [at the time] had the knowledge to judge the merits of Hewitt's observations and the weaknesses of Brinton's" (2007: 80). Today, the assertion that Indian languages lack "true grammatic forms" would be considered racist, but tensions between the informant-become-scholar and others in the discipline continue to arise. Training in an academic field versus apprenticeship in the field, as well as particular training in folklore and related disciplines, had begun to surface, with collectors urged not to presume to interpret their own materials, but to provide data for theorists. Similar issues continue to arise in academic communities today.

By the turn of the twentieth century, emphasis at the Smithsonian had changed from collecting lore to publishing. Although Hewitt continued to go into the field nearly every year, provided copious notes on his sojourns, and continued to publish, the Smithsonian's Charles Walcott in 1909 took him off salary and began to pay him by the number of words he wrote for Bureau of American Ethnology publications. Despite protests, this situation continued until 1914. Throughout his fifty years of employment at the Bureau of American Ethnology, Hewitt was the lowest paid ethnologist, and to date many of his manuscripts remain unpublished.

Zora Neale Hurston

Today, one of the most studied voices of the early twentieth century is that of Zora Neale Hurston. A folklorist herself, she was a student of the famous Boas at a time when women were very much othered in the academy. Further, she was a black woman in a world almost exclusively of white males, so she faced the racial issues that Hewitt faced as well as gender and class issues, since she was from the rural South.

One senses a complicated relationship between Hurston and Boas, since, as a rural, African American woman, she was "supposed" to be the folk, a focus of study at Harvard at that time. Furthermore, she was Boas' student, yet he was dependent on her both as a woman and as a black woman to conduct research that he could not accomplish himself. In a twisted way, he expected her to find evidence to support *his* expectations of what her community might be. Keith Walters writes that Hurston took "revenge" on the white academic establishment in her book, *Mules and Men* (1935), by "starting some shit," like the African American trickster character, the signifying monkey.

While Boas appropriates the work to some extent, validating it in his 1935 preface, her framing is completed by an afterword by another man, Henry Louis Gates, Jr., who wrote, "[Hurston's] barbed critiques were often couched within the tradition of verbal art of the African American community, recognizable by those who read within the traditions" (qtd. in Hurston 2008: 364). Despite this framing of her book by two men, one white and one black, her text dominates, using affective techniques that would have made most ethnographers of her time uncomfortable but that seem remarkably compelling to ethnographers today. Hurston used folktales to confront issues of race and gender, and she used her authorial talents to construct an ethnographic account true to her own deep understanding of and ability to make accessible communal expressive culture.

In doing so, she resisted the pressures of her patrons—her teacher Boas, who treated her as both an informant and an aide, and wealthy white socialite Charlotte Osgood Mason, who supported black artists of the Harlem Renaissance as conduits to understanding America's great link with the so-called primitive. Mason, nearly seventy when she started supporting Hurston's work in the 1920s, owned the intellectual property rights to Hurston's material, an agreement Mason did not demand of male "informants" (Lillios 2010: 47–48).

Anna Lillios (2010) cites scholar Delia Konzett in her observations that the mostly male and city-centered literati considered Hurston's folklore scholarship irrelevant to pressing political issues, overlooking both Hurston's and her "informants'" subtle deployment of counterhegemonic lore. Even though the famous African American writer and activist Langston Hughes traveled to the South with Hurston in the 1920s, he later rather dismissively opined that white folk considered her "the perfect darkie" (Hughes 1940: 239).

Ironically, in the 1920s, some Africans and African Americans were welcomed into the circle of American intellectuals, who had become disillusioned with Western culture after the horrors of World War I, exactly because of certain qualities of folk-ness the African Americans were imagined to possess. Some continued to link "primitivism" to "spiritual and emotional enthusiasm (some would say, soul), indulgence, play, passion, and lust" (Nathan Huggins qtd. in Lillios 2010: 46). The primitive had become "cultural heritage, identity, destiny," still associated with Africa, and still encompassing what was missing from Western civilization, a move that rewarded white scholars, artists, and musicians, but rarely African Americans.

Hurston used expressive culture studies to actively resist embodying what white folk or men expected "primitive" her to be. She was able to confound expectations and be politically counterhegemonic while seeming to conform to what her teachers, patrons, and indeed black men expected of her. In *Mules and Men* she writes, "The white man is always trying to know into somebody else's business. All right, I'll set something outside the door of my mind for him to play with. . . . He can read my writing but he sho' can't read my mind. I'll put this play toy in his hand, and he will seize it and go away. Then I'll say my say and sing my song" (1935: 2). As any tricksterly character must, she takes power from the powerful and makes them appear childlike and impulsive.

WRITING CULTURE

Although Hurston represented *Mules and Men* to Boas, humbly, as a light read for a popular audience—even though subsequent studies have demonstrated definitively the work's complexity—by doing so, she was able to write her way and still gain his introductory one-page nod of approval. She strategically and artistically—"artlessly"—managed to include her credentials as an anthropologist. Near the beginning of *Mules and Men* she writes:

> When I pitched headforemost into the world I landed in the crib of negroism. From the earliest rocking of my cradle, I had known about the capers Br'er Rabbit is apt to cut . . . [b]ut . . . I couldn't see it for wearing it. It was only when I was off in college . . . that I could see myself like somebody else and stand off and look at my garment. Then I had to have the spy-glass of Anthropology. (Hurston 1935: 3)

Unlike her "tight chemise" of negroism, she wore her chemise of anthropology loosely.

I find in her work no fear of "going native," of identifying too closely with her informants, bringing her readers closer to a meaning *full* performance of culture. As a black woman in academia working for a famous man, she had to use strategies we appreciate today. In the postmodern period, ethnographies have become more reflexive (or reflexive field studies have become ethnographies), but that presents problems of its own (to be discussed later).

During the latter half of the twentieth century, attention was paid to the words of women "performers." Elizabeth Warnock Fernea and Basima Bezergan's book, *Middle Eastern Muslim Women Speak*, *Women's Words: The Feminist Practice of Oral History*, by Sherna Gluck and Daphne Patai, or Deborah Kapchan's *Gender on the Market* are examples of different strategies whereby scholars step aside so they and we hear and learn from folk, past and present.

"THAT'S NOT WHAT I SAID"

Whereas Zora Neale Hurston succeeded in part by being both an ethnographer and an informant/performer, Katherine Borland in her article, "'That's Not What I Said.' Interpretive Conflict in Oral Narrative Research" (1991), reflects on issues of scholarly integrity and collaboration with informants in their interpretation of their own stories. Borland recounts a narrative told to her by her Maine grandmother, Beatrice. The story is an entertaining one about a 1944 trip Beatrice had taken to the horse races with her father. Unfortunately, Borland's interpretation falls flat with Beatrice herself. The draft Borland gives her interprets Beatrice's story as one of resistance to male oppression by, for example, placing racing bets against young Beatrice's father's and her hated divorce lawyer's advice. Beatrice's reaction was a fourteen-page letter forcefully resisting the feminist interpretation. At one point she wrote, "You've read into the story what you wished to—what pleases YOU" (1991:70), and contends that the story is no longer hers, but Borland's.

This raises the question: Whose story is it anyway? The stories we all craft about our personal experiences express our worldview. They give us a way of being listened to as we convey multiple messages (that may change radically over time) about how things used to be once upon a time. We would probably feel that our own stories were misinterpreted or important dimensions overlooked, hard as our listener/interpreter might try to get it right. Borland acknowledges that our own current preoccupations influence our understanding of others' narratives. Just as inevitably, the narrator's telling of a story at a particular time and place also affects how she adjusts a story she has probably told many times.

It's instructive to have informants who can talk back, though it makes life difficult. Borland felt that her grandmother's very strong reaction was due to a loss of authorial control. And, I would add that her reaction may have been exacerbated by the feeling that her role as family matriarch was being disrespected. Borland posits what she could have done differently. What probably started off as a simple folklore project demonstrated that, like borrowing money from family members, borrowing stories can cause rifts. All was resolved as Borland was able to work with her grandmother to produce a very fine and nuanced article that discusses the complex relationships that arise between informant and folklorist when issues of hierarchy come into play. She concludes that a more collaborative model can open up for both research partners new ways of understanding the materials and help us avoid falling into the trap of using the expressive culture of others simply as data to support our own research paradigms.

Although this story has a happy ending owing to a developed relationship that could be "stretched to understand the other's perspective,"

(Borland 1991: 74), other scholars have written about folk informants who were so angry that they vowed never again to be interviewed by an ethnographer. Remembering Keith Walters' (1999) article on Hurston, it seems that Walters relistened to Hurston and "collaborated" with her as a tricky ethnographer himself, joining her in writing back against a dominant cadre of white male anthropologists.

The last example gathers up some of the themes we have surveyed in this chapter on folk. The folk figure Salam Pax is very much betwixt and between. In his blog, issues of agency arise as he carves out a place and claims a voice, challenging personal and authority categories in ways we encountered with Hurston, Hewitt, Du Bois, Appiah, Fabian, and others. Furthermore, like Hurston and Burton, he is something of a trickster with a performance that eludes any attempt to find it a generic safe haven.

Salam's blog is a gigantic, choppy, personal experience narrative told to a global folk group that includes people who can coalesce around knowledge of global pop culture, gay cultures, local Islams, Arabic dialects, Arab cultures (especially urban), Arab hi(stories) versus Western hi(stories), and youth culture. The blog begins and focuses on the impending U.S. invasion of Iraq in March 2003 and continues on for some months after the invasion takes place. Salam is a twenty-something intent on living his life even in the midst of chaos. The blog isn't a coming-of-age piece emerging from war, like Anne Frank's, to whom Gawker Media's Nick Denton compared Salam. He is not the War's Elvis either, as Peter Maas of *Slate.com* suggests, despite their shared trickster characteristics.

Rather, Salam's blog is like episodes of the TV show *Friends*, if *Friends* had been narrated by one person with an extended family and much scarier problems than the typical twenty-something predicaments in the TV sitcom. Let us look at Salam as a folk figure, a trickster, someone who "embodies" a disbursed folk community, and someone who, like Hurston, takes a verbal, humorous revenge on the powers that be. Like the Arab trickster Juha, Salam's seemingly harmless behavior troubles certain assumptions about reality. Salam interrogates and undermines both mainstream media and scholarly analyses of Iraqi otherness. Adapting Basil Bernstein's (1971) theory of language codes, I suggest that Salam's blog draws on a restricted language code drawn upon by intimate folk communities with closely shared assumptions and understandings, rather than an elaborated one needed for less cohesive audiences.

As Walters says of Hurston, Salam writes outside the scholarly, or in his case, journalistic, tradition. He tricks us into finding a commonality with Iraqis. Salam does not recount horror stories about the war or display photos of dead bodies but rather does an end-run around the "usual channels" of reportage drawing on what Walters (1999: 344), referring to Henry Louis Gates, calls a "speakerly text." He uses the illusion of oral chatting to confound various powerful entities that affect him—real powers like George W. Bush and Saddam Hussein, but also powers of fear, want, and despair. His blog performance is full of speech play and verbal art. The joking, mocking irony brings us into his home and into the streets, and only intermittently do we realize the horrors we are laughing through. He confounds categories—folk, pop, establishment, spoken/written, East/West, gay/straight youth/adult— and uses Arablish (an amalgam of Arabic and English) to reshape his own identity as he and his readers negotiate Iraqi-ness. His blog, *Where Is Raed* (dear_raed.blogspot.com) morphs for his readers into where and who Salam Pax is.

Folklore can play havoc with the folklorist's agency to define (or confine) genres and folk groups, complicating the meaning and use of these classifications. Folklore in the blogosphere raises questions about how stable a folk group must be to qualify as one, and about genre boundaries—where any genre starts and ends. Most of us belong to multiple folk groups, some with a solid core and wandering peripheries and some almost too fluid or fleeting to grasp. At first, Salam Pax participated unreflexively in reportage, endeavoring simply to stay connected to his global folk community of late twenty-somethings and especially his friend Raed (studying in Jordan and not good at answering email). And, he was delighted that his group was growing. But finally the people who "speak the same language(s)," were invaded, shortly after the actual invasion, by an "outsider" audience intent on either discovering who he was (capturing him, figuratively or literally) or fitting him into a politically less troublesome slot. The pressure effectively destroyed the folk community qua community, although it may have served its purpose.

CONCLUSION

As we have seen in this chapter, definitions of both folk and folklorists are complicated and unstable. This situation charms and confounds. New media make spaces for folk voices previously muted to be profoundly influential—appreciated and attended to by multiple audiences over time. Throughout the remainder of the book we will touch on the difficult ethical challenges we face, as creative individuals share their insights with us folklorists.

Chapter Five

Performance

The emergent quality of performance resides in the interplay between communicative resources, individual competence, and the goals of the participants, within the context of particular situations.
        — Richard Bauman, *Verbal Art as Performance*

Occasionally, a scholar pauses to reconsider a cluster of attributes that have contributed to a certain scholarly endeavor and how that work has generated a spate of new insights. In 1974 folklorist Richard Bauman published a fifty-page working paper in sociolinguistics, which built on principles derived from "conversation" among linguistic anthropologists, sociolinguists, and folklorists as well as philosophers, sociologists, and literati. In the paper, "Verbal Art as Performance" (later published as a book), Bauman summed up work in which scholars began to see the efficacy of studying folklore as "performed." Bauman, "starting as a folklorist," calls attention to the "integrative tradition" from "at least the time of Herder" that coalesced around attention to the performance of verbal art. As he wrote twelve years later:

> A large part of my own agenda in investigating the poetics of performance stems from a conviction that whatever anthropology, folklore, and linguistics have gained from the modern pursuit of disciplinary autonomy has come at the sacrifice of the unified vision of language, art, and society that constitutes our common intellectual heritage. The poetics of performance, I submit, can provide a powerful integrative frame of reference for the next stage of our inquiry into that most fundamental and fascinating of all problems–the art of life itself. (Bauman 1986: 148)

A focus on performance in folklore studies helps loosen disciplinary and genre bonds (whether etic or emic) that might have been productive during the modernist moment but inhibit a full appreciation of the versatility and poetics or aesthetics of lore in performance.

Like folkloristics itself, the idea of verbal art as performance reaches into both literary and social science fields. That inspiration owes much to the work of linguist Roman Jakobson, whose research focused on literature and language in cultural context. Dell Hymes was a linguistic anthropologist like Bauman, and his later work focused on the poetics of performance or ethnopoetics. Both Hymes and Jakobson tended toward aesthetically informed projects that resonate with Bauman's insights about performance.

In this chapter we look at performance theory as it relates to folklore and how that approach to folkloristics has opened up possibilities for the field today in at least four interrelated ways: by emphasizing the centrality (by definition) of aesthetics to lore; by lessening the need to be tied to specific genres when speaking of lore; by attending to the role of the "audience" in negotiating the "aesthetics" of lore and hence its emergent, communal, quality; and by moving away from the need to use literary evaluative touchstones to unpack nonliterary lore like customary practices and material culture. Attention to the "poetics of performance" in folklore studies would open up a broader semiotic system that did not privilege literary theory or methodology, one that allows for alternative aesthetic moments and designs with which to study the artistry of folk performances (like material culture production) that may not foreground language. Concerning this broadening of lore to include other than verbal art, Bauman writes:

> I proposed a definition of performance as the assumption of accountability to an audience for a display of communicative competence, subject to evaluation for the relative skill and effectiveness by which the act of communication is accomplished, above and beyond the other communicative functions of the verbal utterance. Now, although this initial formulation was developed with specific reference to verbal performance, I would like here to suggest that the *notion is in fact generalizable to other semiotic systems, that is to other communicative codes* (1986: 142–143; emphasis added).

For the purposes of folklore, we need to remember two things: We need a folk audience participating/evaluating, and the performance must inspire aesthetic or poetic (both broadly defined) evaluation.

"BREAKTHROUGH INTO PERFORMANCE"

"Breakthrough into Performance" can refer to the moment when rich possibilities for focusing on the poetics of folk performances began to be recognized. In Hymes' (1975) terms, it refers to that moment when ordinary conversation is transformed by an individual or group into an event that calls for heightened attention. Folk performer(s) and their audiences elicit particular notice in performance-based studies. This is quite different from early days, when the folk artist was more likely to be treated as a vessel for lore, to be emptied and forgotten and the only audiences of interest tended to be other researchers.

Lore as Emergent

In "Breakthrough into Performance" (1975) Hymes offers his strategies for studying speech events as a useful way to understand how such events are both fashioned within the parameters of particular cultural systems while concurrently altering, with the collaboration of an audience, those same systems. Hymes and Bauman lured anthropologists and others into recognizing the importance of individual actions that involve heightened affect. Such "performances" indicate that the speaker feels the topic is worthy of aesthetic crafting in order to catch the attention and approval of an audience of one or many, near or distant or both. At the same time, Hymes hoped that

> folklore would take the lead in showing how appreciation and interpretation of performances as unique events can be united with analysis of the underlying rules and regularities which make performances possible and intelligible; in showing how to overcome the divorce between the emergent and the repeatable, between the actual, the realizable, and the systemically possible that has plagued the study of speech. (1975: 11)

Indeed, this performance concept was quickly taken up and further elaborated. Dundes' concept of text, texture, and context was rendered under this rubric more complex and less subject to the strictures of genres or media. And, folklorists also quickly opened up "performance" to include events that were not, or not only, verbal but that could be musical, involve material culture, and depend on more than one medium and genre within a frame recognized by both speaker and audience as performative.

Once the performer has "taken the floor" and engaged the audience, that audience expects communicative competence that will provide an enhanced and affecting experience that transcends simple communication. At the same time, the audience is free to evaluate the intrinsic qualities of the act as aesthetically persuasive, appropriate, and insightful, at least within a particular folk community. Bauman notes, "Performance thus calls forth special attention to and heightened awareness of the act of expression and gives license to the audience to regard the act of expression and the performer with special intensity" (1977: 11).

This acknowledgment by Bauman of a framed event that is intentionally interpretive is a great help when one is working to circumscribe what can be called folklore—especially when the boundary between the

inside and outside of a folk phenomenon is too fluid to fit comfortably
into even a very accommodating genre, like festival. But the central nug-
get in Bauman's reperception of folklore as a performance of communal
affect is the articulation of an audience's right to evaluate *aesthetically*
the communicator's performance and the communicator's usually unspo-
ken acknowledgment that she or he can thus be evaluated.

An example is a riddle-telling session I recorded of some young
men in a Mediterranean town in Tunisia in 1974. The single, twenty-
somethings were telling riddles in Tunisian Arabic, riddles pertaining
to some aspect of life in the town. One youth came in from hunting with
his hawk, a practice in the region at least since Roman occupation two
thousand years earlier, hawk perched on his shoulder. His riddle was
"A (gentle)man came from the North, You don't know who he is, On his
feet yellow leather slides, On his back a black wool cloak." The answer
is the (black and yellow) sparrow hawk that migrates to town from
across the Mediterranean.

After several of these riddles with answers pertinent to the town
(beehives, whitewash, the local bus, henna) another young man took
the floor to tell a riddle in classical Arabic, but was brushed off by the
others. Even though in many circumstances a classical riddle would
have been considered more aesthetically pleasing, more charming, in
this context his offering fell flat. All the young men offering riddles
were performing and being evaluated at some level, but one performance failed with this audience, in this time and place.

Audience as Emergent?

It's not simple to determine how the breakthrough (into performance) is precipitated or what a folk community is. Who calls for that
heightened attention? A member of the group might ask for a story—
either because the performer is known to be a competent performer or
because the story is one the listener likes. Who decides what is worthy?
We might encounter a glassblower to admire, or perhaps a pizza chef
tossing pizza dough high in the air or catching it with a special flourish.
In those cases we might be lookers-on with no particular connections to
the crafts or ability to evaluate them as members of the folk group might.

From chapter 4, recall that Becker was walking in Zanzibar when
his attention was called to a musical (and perhaps sensory) performance,
an "intimate concert" as coffee beans were ground by pestles rhythmi-
cally hitting cast-iron mortars. In this example, sustained performance
depends on the participation of a folk group of women as both audience
and performers, communicating with an unseen audience, at least one of
whom, Becker, was from another continent. But he was able to find common aesthetic ground (sound) with the "other," the ladies of Zanzibar.

Becker has passed that possibility of audience appreciation on to
us. How does the account of this long-ago and faraway performance

affect us as audience? What does such a performance have in common with a casual verbal duel? Analysis of performances requires study of a complex, negotiated, intermingling of performers and audiences amongst whom such events may be reworked for years to come. Sometimes the audience is exoteric (onlookers or listeners), sometimes esoteric (members of the folk group), but sometimes also complicated intermixes. Performance depends for its meaning on an audience, though not necessarily an audience that is present at the time of the performance. As in the case of graffiti or the piecing of a quilt, lore can invoke a future, absent or imagined audience.

Being open to the multiple ways a breakthrough occurs makes it easy to see that recognition of a folk performance depends on often spontaneous negotiation between audience(s) and performer(s). That a performance has occurred might not even be recognized until after the fact. The bucolic wit's saying, "When the wine's in the wit's out," surely must be fully heard and absorbed to be appreciated. Even the contrast between the literal (wine's in) and the metaphorical (wit's out) might not be fully grasped until a recap the next day, when presumably the wine would also be "out" and mental acuity improved. The performer might even claim entitlement to an aesthetically constructed event after the fact, for example, by remarking, "no pun intended," whether or not the pun was, in fact, unintended.

Within a folk community, what counts as a performance can be a brief, well-turned, phrase, a joke, a proverb, or the performance of an epic over several nights in a coffee house. It can be the throwing of a pot, a move in a basketball game, "excessive celebration," or a local history narrative. These events stop the flow of everyday life and claim for a time entitlement to the special attention of a communal audience. These are breakthroughs into performance.

As suggested in chapter 3, "performance," as a methodological tool for the study of folklore typically has very little to do with staged performances, and, in fact, is often their antithesis, better described as grassroots-managed aesthetic or expressive culture. Once folklore loses its counterhegemonic edginess, its communal changeability and flexibility, I see it nudging along a continuum toward more frozen popular culture.

PERFORMING DIFFERENCE

Folklorist Yuanhao (Graham) Zhao compares the staged performance of minorities in China with the grassroots performances of the Chinese Hui minority. Staged celebrations of Chinese-ness, like the New Year celebration televised all over China and beyond, attempt to recognize and represent dozens of Chinese minorities. The solution is to dress each of the fifty-plus minorities in clothing stereotypical of that minority. The Hui are represented in "Hui-like" costumes (strange to most Hui), dancing and singing and carrying folksy Hui artifacts. While this might be a popular idea of how the folkness of minorities should be represented (reminiscent of singing, dancing throngs), Zhao assures me that Hui are not particularly "into" singing and dancing. While a scholar of performance studies might study Chinese stage(d) performances such as these, such performances are not fundamental to folklore studies. (See Deborah Kapchan, especially the 1995 article on performance.)

A folklorist's attention is drawn to communal performances that are rarely staged and may have little to do with outsiders. We might think of a Thanksgiving celebration where the same people (family or not) gather year after year. We could think of this as a little tradition (opposed to a "great tradition" or master narrative of Thanksgiving-ness) wherein a group of people have worked out what needs to happen to make their event successfully "Thanksgiving-like": particular food, who prepares it, where the event takes place, how much focus is put on giving thanks and for what, the role of genders and ages from youth to seniors. Unless someone new is invited to participate, the celebration is not foregrounded as a performance of difference. Noticing how another group of celebrants down the street or on NPR performs the specialness of the day is not likely to be as important as negotiations within the group about what feels right for Thanksgiving.

But for the Hui and other minorities, expressive culture is an important resource to draw on within their own folk groups, as well as to meaningfully maintain their own identities vis-à-vis the majority Han. (A parallel could be drawn with Native Americans in Canada who, for the opening ceremony of the Winter Olympics in 2010, sang and danced wearing special costumes. However beautifully, they were neatly contained within their stereotype.) Then how do the Hui perform Hui-ness in the folkloristic sense? How do minorities intermingled with a vast majority draw on folklore to make a space for themselves, if it is not by singing special songs, dancing folk dances, or donning special costumes meant to set them apart?

At a grassroots level, for both the Hui Muslim minority and the Han non-Muslim majority, an important locus of difference is Muslim abstinence from pork—a widely preferred meat source in China—and so a marker of difference every day that could at any moment draw attention. For example, snacks are passed out to children in schools, and Muslim children are given pork-free snacks, marking them as different. Some of these performances of Hui foodways are visual—special signs often with a picture of a pitcher and words, sometimes in Arabic or Arabic-looking script, that advertise a pork-free space to dine—whether a simple push cart or a fine restaurant. The pitcher in itself is not a "performance," but in this context it performs "Muslim-ness" for viewers.

Martha Sims and Martine Stephens (2005) offer other examples of visuals that represent customary practices of folk groups—a horse-shoe hung over a doorway or the Asian practice of *feng shui*, arranging household items in felicitous ways. A horseshoe properly hung over a doorway becomes more than a horseshoe; it becomes an indicator of a folk idea that it holds good luck in the house.

Likewise, a representation of a pitcher can be read variously by Hui or Han as a compressed performance of Muslim-ness, represent-ing, along with the Arabic or fake Arabic writing surrounding it, a history of the arrival of Muslims in China, the ablutions that Hui do before their five-times-a-day prayers, the cleanliness of Hui food, and, of course, the absence of pork. Enhancing the message of the multi-vocalic sign is the food performance, demanding special attention in presentation, taste, and scent. As Sims and Stephenson write, "When we read an object or practice in this way, we are . . . analyzing its per-formance—what it communicates actively to the world, both within and outside the folk groups that created it (esoterically [Hui], and exo-terically [Han and other, non-Hui Chinese])" (2005: 135). They add, "The performance approach establishes folklore as current, evolving and always expressive—regardless of the type of text we analyze (136).

Performance of Huiness may also emerge under provocation. Zhao recounts a preadolescent fight with a Han schoolmate. Although the fight itself had no audience and did not go well, Zhao embellishes it with an artfully crafted personal experience narrative:

> *Experience I: Your ancestors are pigs!*
> *Setting*: On the schoolyard of my elementary school.
> *Participants*: Three elementary school children, including one from the Han majority (10 or 11 years old), two from the Hui (me, about 10 years old; an acquaintance of about 10 or 11 years old).
> *Scene*: When I was about 10 years old, there was once a quarrel between one of my Han classmates and me. The quarrel didn't start out to be about pork; it was another issue that had nothing to do with pork, religion, or "ethnicity," but then for some reason it escalated to pork. I, however, have forgotten what the trigger was. Conflict in words elevated to conflict in body; my classmate was taller than me, so he clutched my neck so I couldn't reach him, then he said: "Do you know why the Hui people do not eat pork? Because your ancestors are pigs!" I was so angry that I tried to kick him. Dramatically, another Hui student in my class passed by, and I yelled to him, "He said the Hui people's ancestors are pigs, help me beat him up!" The classmate fighting with me turned to the Hui passerby and said, "No, I just mean his (meaning my) ances-tors are pigs, not yours." Then that Hui passerby nodded and left!

I was desperate and I yelled: "We are all Hui people! My ancestors are yours!" But he wouldn't listen to me. I have forgotten when the fight ended or how.

Every time Zhao tells the story, it elicits laughter. It is well-crafted, and like all folk performances, it takes considerable time to critique. We could argue that the fight was also a performance, but just as every battle needs a raconteur to make it meaningful and memorable, so are the meanings for the street fight carried in stories about it. In a sense, the fight ends twenty years later with Zhao the winner.

If the performance is subject to evaluation, of course it is subject to multiple evaluations, but unlike Amy Shuman's fight stories in *Storytelling Rights*, where there is some dueling over who has the right to tell the story, Zhao owns this story. Zhao's fight story is, like the pitcher display, evaluated differently in different contexts, and it is evaluated in terms of its aesthetic appeal rather than its veracity. We imagine the frustration of the child and his relief when he sees a fellow Hui approaching only to be confounded again, eliciting more laughter from the audience, as the other Hui youth accepts the argument that one Hui's ancestors are pigs and another's are not.

Arguably, the young Turks' most significant contribution to ethnography and art in their attention to performative resources was to "unpack" the "affective" dimension of lore, to demonstrate and convey to outsiders how a community's expressive culture provides a centripetal force that sustains community in good times and bad—war, natural disasters, colonialism, global hegemony. For those who bring a sophisticated understanding of the Hui group to the performance, Zhao's appeal to the other Hui youth can be understood as drawing on a central maxim that is part of that sustenance for Hui, "All Hui under heaven are one family," a maxim that is ignored by the other Hui child. As illustrated here, because folklore represents one of the *performative* dimensions of culture, it sometimes packs a rhetorical punch out of proportion to its apparent everydayness. Thus, transformational power of work songs, or puppet street theater, or jokes, with their sometimes stealthy attacks on the status quo, can go unrecognized as such and unsanctioned.

MATERIAL CULTURE AS PERFORMANCE

One might ask how much a barn raising or other nonverbal event can also claim status as a communal folk performance. Sometimes museums refer to the assemblage of material culture items in their exhibitions as "performances," and we can very much look at Bastian's attempts to organize his museums as performances: either scientific, illustrative of cultural diffusion or the "ascent of man," or artistic, moving from simple to more complex examples of folk artistry—both from a European perspective (Hicks 2010). But what about performance in the production and use of material culture by us folk? Items do not "break through" into performance, but the collection and display of material culture items in our homes can perform, with or without added commentary, an assessment of what to celebrate about the past, present, and future. My mother-in-law has carefully displayed in her living room mementos of times past and folk communities long dispersed. Marking occasions on her walls, besides photographs, are paintings and poems, her own and others that she has accumulated over the years.

The words and images represent what she holds dear in the celebration of peaceful nature—waking up to a snowy day, cows grazing in a field, a river scene. These items call forth layers of memories—inspected one by one or by how they are grouped. She, who was once the audience, now performs her story for a new audience—guests in her home. As a young bride, she had watched her mother-in-law piecing a quilt and much later became the audience as her sister-in-law's sewing circle quilted it. Having heard tales of the "ingredients" of the quilt—the fabrics, stitches, talents, and personalities of the quilters—she becomes the performer as she elaborates the story of the quilt to a new audience.

Such performances negotiate how layers of meaning accrue around the item—nostalgia for lost arts or a loved one with clever hands now stilled, admiration for certain patterns or needlework, celebration of a community that fashions good work, the context in which the item was produced ("working after dinner, listening to the radio, sitting in this very chair" or with a community of sewers not always harmonious). The reinvention may even become a "virtue out of necessity" story, wherein the teller is pleased that she now has a larger choice of where to put her time and talents, since quilts can now be made by machine or bought in a store. Text, texture, and context—material, verbal, visual, oral, and aural—coalesce around the object in the process of being fashioned as product. The performance is dependent on material and voice; otherwise, as Simon Penny remarks about the link between technology and art, the "chain of attribution to the originator" is broken, erasing "meaningful social flows" (147).

Pat Mullen describes the "meaningful social flows" related to a barn raising performed in Adams County, Ohio, in 1858 (Webber and Mullen 2011). In 1980, it was Mr. Glasgow, the 87-year-old grandson of the owner of the barn, who shared with Mullen a very affecting story of the barn's progress. He relates in loving detail the work of raising the 120-year-old barn—the man who hammered out the hinges and nails for the barn, the fifty-three pieces of timber, hand-hewn by Sam Laird, "a craftsman, honey, he wasn't no ordinary carpenter."

But Glasgow also tells the dramatic story of the day of the barn raising, comparing the communal effort of raising the barn to that of another kind of performance, the folk dances that would occur after the work was done. Laird was a caller for the barn raising like the caller for a dance, Glasgow says. All was going well until one young man didn't pull his weight and the heavy timber slipped. Laird calls him a "lazy lout," the lad panics and moves too quickly, and before Laird can move his hand the timber comes down on the end of his thumb and smashes it between the heavy timbers. Dramatically, Laird keeps on orchestrating the barn raising for another twenty minutes, finishing the job while masking his agony.

The story, in Glasgow's telling, illustrates the importance of community cooperation, and Glasgow remarks that Laird had endured just deserts for his harsh words to the young man. Laird's thumb remains today a part of the barn. Obviously, material objects do not "break through" into performance as a storyteller might, but "[m]aterial culture offers other advantages over words alone. For example, objects are less ephemeral. . . . Their materiality makes them well suited for display, and having survived from the past grants them authority to bear witness" (Cashman 2008: 148). A folk dance, a barn raising, folk music, a tale: performative success depends on how sight, sound, and touch and on how text, texture, and context are incorporated by their creators or interpreters.

Although we are all the folk, we are not at any given moment drawing on the expressive culture resources available to us in our various folk communities. Sitting in class these days we can no longer engage, as audience or actor, in the performance, watched covertly but raptly by all but the hapless girl (and, one hopes, the teacher), of the folk practice of stealthily dipping a girl's pigtail in the inkwell; the art of producing and disbursing spitballs seem to be similarly less practiced these days (although they are for sale, and there are directions for making them online). Some settings are more conducive to folk performances than others, and classrooms formally resist, but in resisting somehow also foster, at least among certain age groups, the desire to upset the status quo—with spitballs or tacks on chairs. These small uprisings—folk performances or folk pranks—are not centrally dependent on language but rather on silence and stealth. In such cases, the performance depends on active, engaged, barely contained silence on the part of the folk community of students within a particular classroom and an "anti-audience" of adults in authority.

While the notion of genre remains useful, performance studies allow us to look at lore from an alternative interpretive frame (see Goffman 1974), especially helpful when communal and aesthetic dimensions do not fit neatly into a genre slot. Performance studies call attention to process as well as product and make room for a hodgepodge of happenings that cross media (visual, verbal, musical) and generic boundaries—including bits that we could only artificially force into some generic classification. Furthermore, an alternative framework for interpretation is useful in avoiding appropriation by the looky-loos, spectators outside the folk group (Hickey 1997). As Edward M. Bruner and Barbara Kirshenblatt-Gimblett (1994), Susan Slyomovics (1998), and others have observed, performances are politicized—"appropriated, commodified, and essentialized" (Kapchan 2003: 133). Where appropriated, they, often in generic form, become culture writ small, stripped of much of their multivocality.

Thus, folk communities tend to make their expressive culture forms more amorphous and less easy for outsiders to gather neatly, stripped of essential contexts, simplified and sanitized perhaps for use in a television commercial (using jump rope performances to advertise chewing gum) or on a greeting card. I am *not* convinced that performative identities, especially public ones, always depend on and define, or are defined by, a genre. As I speculated earlier, sometimes performative agency depends on eluding genre and on confounding expectations, or perhaps one could think of these performances as signaling emergent genres (see chapter 7).

Folklore (whether verbal, material, or both) is compressed culture that invites and rewards careful attention and analysis. This is not surprising to most folklorists, but scholars even in closely related disciplines are often confused about the difference between "folklore" and "culture." Of course folklore is a dimension of culture, and the terms are permeable to some extent, but the value of attending to culture that a community has taken the time to craft affectively is immense. Simply put, considerations of text, texture, and context are necessary but not sufficient factors in trying to understand why, for any group, some cultural events comment more effectively than others on who we are and where we should be going.

FOLKLORE AND CULTURAL CAPITAL

Bauman enabled folklorists to recognize that folk performances depend to a greater degree than other kinds of performance on a negotiation between performers and audience. That negotiation takes place over the finer points of their shared culture as well as strategies or resources to re-form or otherwise respond to "what else is out there." The reward of the culture broker/performer in a private or semiprivate occasion is not monetary but rather a wealth of communal appreciation. Perhaps we should avoid the Econ. 101 metaphor here, but "cultural capital" is an apt description for what, for example, a witty or outrageous guy owns, "bought" with an artistic way with words, clever comebacks, or savvy behaviors recounted over days, if not years, among the people he hangs out with.

Years ago, I attended a wedding in a small town in the Maghrib. As was usual, the women in the women-only section were urging each other to get up and dance. It was truly a breakthrough into performance when a thin, simply dressed, middle-aged poor relation of the well-off family of the bride got up and began to dance. We were stunned by the transformation, by the amount of energy and artistry of that seemingly "ordinary" little body. As the other women heaped encouragement and compliments on her, for the length of the dance the bride and the wedding were quite forgotten. She had an unexpected resource, all the more powerful for that unexpectedness.

Other kinds of cultural capital can pay off monetarily. A townsman and his brother from that same small town traveled by camel between the Mediterranean and Sahara in the late 1930s selling goods and acquiring more to sell along the way. He was known as a riddler, and his business flourished partly due to his reputation as a verbal artist. People in the hinterland waited to do business with him (as opposed to other "traveling salesmen") due to his clever poem-riddles.

There is nothing self-aggrandizing about any of these performances; any aggrandizing that takes place must come from reportage about the performers, which, if cleverly done, then might add another layer of artfulness.

ORALITY AND LITERACY

Folklore, perhaps more than any other discipline, has been disadvantaged by the quest for disciplinary autonomy that has characterized modern scholarship. . . . In particular, folklorists have been wrenched by the counter-pulls of . . . the humanities and the social sciences, which have threatened the unified frame of reference that was folklore's foundation.

— Richard Bauman, "Performance and Honor
in 13th-Century Iceland"

In "Performance and Honor in 13th-Century Iceland" (1986), Bauman argues for recognition of "performance domains," that is, cultural domains that, to work, depend on aesthetic performances. Who was honorable (possessing "manly virtues" of valor, hospitality, eloquence, self-possession) had to be communally, publically, and artfully negotiated. Although the domain, honor, was not contested as a desirable quality, what counted as honorable behavior and who counted depended on artful, public performances—process rather than product—and that process depended on a semiotic system, integrating verbal art and honor organized around performance.

Such semiotic approaches offer folklorists and others who specialize in expressive culture studies the possibility of refocusing on performers and audiences as they draw on a broad spectrum of culturally situated analytical resources, and as they speak to concerns shared with scholars in the humanities and social sciences and beyond. Hence, we can better study the strong aesthetic links between communal values and communal art that folk communities achieve through their inventive marshaling of multiple media and genres. This melding of disciplinary insights and concerns can offer complex appreciations of folklore in new media and provide guidelines for approaching the expressive culture found, for example, in the Salam Pax blog, which exists somewhere between orality and literacy.

Attention to cultural affect's centrality to the rhetorical power of lore, from Icelandic sagas to Salam's blog, yields fundamental insight into how folk groups define and redefine themselves vis-à-vis externally imposed folk group categories such as nationality, ethnicity, occupation, age, religion, and so on. Further, folklorists are able to analyze how any particular group emerges and how the criteria for membership are expressively negotiated.

Bauman posits convincingly that "honor" is a performance domain in thirteenth-century Iceland. I posit that Salam, although very much involved in constructing himself as an Iraqi icon, would, like comedian Dick Gregory in his trickster persona, rather be a live coward than a dead hero. I would argue that both Salam in his blog and Zora Neale Hurston in *Mules and Men* construct themselves not as heroes but as tricksters—antiheroes who draw on folklore, that is, communal expressivity, to challenge hegemonic "truths." Like Gregory, they redefine what's at stake by deploying tricky language to offset their social vulnerabilities.

Bauman points out that folklorists have produced a suggestive body of ethnographic work that argues convincingly for the inclusion of an aesthetically grounded performance component in any attempt to comprehend how claims to moral worth are communicatively accomplished and recognized in the conduct of social life whatever may be the social structural and economic foundations and results of such performances." (1986: 146–47). Salam's blog is not ethnography, but it is, I suggest, an aesthetically grounded folk performance with claims, no matter how outrageously proffered, to worth. Layers of folklore emerge so that Salam becomes a folk figure, a trickster, a legendary character endowed by his group with extra-regional gravitas. With a strategy resembling Gregory's, he mixes his role as social critic/activist with appealingly outrageous behavior. At the same time, U.S., Iraqi, and Israeli journalists, regional officialdom, and intelligence groups try to pull him back into their game and make him conform to their discourse, which is almost the antithesis of his unfettered self-definition. As this new shadowy audience becomes evident, Salam makes them part of his banter, but in the end the dike is breached, and, as we will see in the last chapter, the world he created with his community is flooded.

CONCLUSION

Taking account of performance in folklore studies, really looking closely at the aesthetic or expressive dimension of lore in all its contexts, is more important today than ever. Cultural coherence does not depend on anything more than a group's expressive resources. Students of lore need to know the performer(s) and the audience(s), and what is brought to the performance occasion in terms of their shared histories. What has led up to a particular aesthetically charged moment? How do performer(s) and audience(s) build on that past to comment on the present and negotiate for the future drawing on their shared poetics of performance? Such moments become powerful tools for acknowledging and resisting global and local inequities.

Chapter Six

Comparative Folklore

Who would have imagined that the obscure and technical details of the land tenure of the aboriginal tribes of India could shed any light upon the condition of Ireland?

— E. S. Hartland, *Folklore: What Is It and What Is the Good of It?*

The need is becoming apparent for a new comparative perspective which seeks to discover why folklore should take different forms, serve different functions, and enjoy different degrees of importance in social life from culture to culture, and this calls for its investigation as an integral part of larger sociocultural and behavioral systems.

— Richard Bauman, "Quaker Folk-Linguistics and Folklore"

The oldest, and still perhaps the most common, technique of folklore analysis is comparison.

— Jan Harold Brunvand, *The Study of American Folklore*

In his now classic *The Study of American Folklore* (1968), Jan Brunvand notes that one goal of comparative research for American folklorists is to "bring their viewpoint to bear on other closely related scholarly fields" (35). Comparative folklore projects were taken up in the late nineteenth century when comparative projects were still the *sine qua non* for "scientific" studies. Thus, folklorists have continued to produce methodologies for global comparison of verbal art, like folktales and motifs, or other intangibles like religious systems, as we saw with Müller, or language and song that echo systems used by geologists or biologists for classifying tangibles (for example, Linnaeus' plant classification system of genus and species).

Other comparative projects have been messier. They have disrupted the neatness of abstract, Eurocentric sciences and challenged the assumed social hierarchies resisting, artfully, the scientistic effort to systematize the world. These projects have remained one resource for challenging, from within, reified and thus almost invisible structures of social power. They can "make strange" cultural phenomena that ordinarily are taken for granted or call into question assumed communal or global hierarchies. We have seen examples of this disturbance—often initiated by white men themselves—of assumptions about classification and hierarchization earlier. Orchard's comparison of Native Americans' and Anglo Americans' preference for rare components in their artistic projects put their cultural practices on an equal footing, as did his comparison of the similar standards by which Anglo embroidery and Native American quill art are likely to be judged.

We see categories in disarray, too, in Dundes' comparison of football habits with homoeroticism, or Clodd's linking of Catholic and pagan rituals. Hurston complained that Boas did not want her to write about similarities between Christian and Voodoo rituals. Much of Burton's trickster reputation came from his challenges to existing hierarchies, as when he compared Oxford University professors unfavorably to teachers at the Al-Azhar Mosque in Cairo.

E. S. Hartland, in his 1904 book, *Folklore: What Is It and What Is It Good For?*, argued for comparative studies of global lore. An understanding of the folk laws governing land use in India would have shed light on the Irish system, he laments, but instead, "We went in with a rough hand and broke up the fabric of Irish society. . . . Elizabethan lawyers were utterly ignorant of any system of law except their own" (29). In this case, Hartland argues for the practicality of a comparative study of two geographically distant locals, a practice that Pat Mullen and I (2011) suggest continues to offer insight today.

Privileging the Western project of comparison and categorization is, as Michel Foucault argues, a powerful way "science" is manipulated to impose social control by those able to "establish the system of identities and the order of differences" (2003: 27) among seemingly "natural" entities. However, comparison, if used creatively, may jar systems of organization that powerful entities have an interest in reifying. Folklore, by definition, deployed "locally," communally, and expressively, is an important locus for this counterhegemonic type of comparison.

Early scientific strategies of comparison of lore were based on parallel systems for plants, animals (including Homo sapiens), and minerals established early in the eighteenth century. These generally relied not on in-depth ethnographic studies of particular communities but on massive surveys that then classified and compared across time and space. Even scientists who studied manners and customs in their travels were typically more ethnological than ethnographic, skimming across many surfaces rather than developing in-depth studies of any one region.

This area-studies approach blurred early disciplinary boundaries so that, for example, Sir Richard happily gathered during his travels not only folklore and languages but flora, fauna and material culture, as did his acquaintance, Robert Bruce Napoleon Walker, who spent much of his life working in West Africa as a representative of a trading firm based in Liverpool. His son by Agñorogoulé Ikoutou of the Mpongwe tribe of the Gabon Estuary, became the first Gabonese Roman Catholic priest, Monseigneur André Raponda-Walker, an author, ethnographer, and botanist, whose books on Gabonese folklore covered rituals and beliefs, folk medicine, and stories. His comparative work sometimes drew on local anecdotes that troubled the assumptions of Western missionaries, scientists, and travelers about their innate superiority. In one account, Raponda-Walker, drawing on his position as what today would be dubbed a "halfie"—one "whose national or cultural identity is mixed by virtue of migration, overseas education, or parentage" (Abu-Lughod 1991: 137), implicitly allies himself with an African grandma. He recounts in *Souvenirs d'un nonagénaire* (1993) watching her squirt her breast milk into the face of a French missionary priest when he informed her that she could not possibly nurse her baby granddaughter.

As we have already seen in chapter 4 in regard to folk like Hewitt and Hurston, people socially, ethnically, culturally "betwixt and between" can "embody" a challenge to assumed hierarchies of knowledge and power. In her work, *Imperial Eyes* (1992), Mary Louise Pratt observes: "Natural history extracted specimens not only from their organic or ecological relations with each other, but also from their places in other peoples' economies, histories, social and symbolic systems" (31). So it was with folklore "specimens"— whether constructed objects like shields or intangibles like folktales. Plant and animal specimens were often collected without interest in how they might have been used in situ for folk medicine, dyes, or adornment. These classificatory projects, Pratt notes, had earlier been undertaken alongside broader studies of local knowledges but functioned in the Imperial era as yet another form of domination.

Some linguists and philologists did work in the field to classify and compare languages within the confines of certain regions, often for diffusion studies. This work was more grounded in local interrelationships and contexts, but it was no less colonial. Nevertheless, these more situated studies could sometimes escape the suspect armchair linguistics of scholars like Brinton, whose comparisons of Native American languages led him to conclude that those languages were inferior to European languages. And yet, these regional diffusion projects faced setbacks brought on by the very imperialist ambitions that enabled and fostered them. Bastian's desire, for example, to study the diffusion of material culture, was thwarted as the colonizing nations in the Pacific (Germany, the U.S., Spain, the Netherlands, and France), each possessively guarded its territory.

MOTIF AND TALE-TYPE INDEXES:
METHODS FOR STUDYING THE "DEVELOPMENT"
OF FOLKTALES (*MÄRCHEN*)

Lore was collected and classified, and commonalities were noted by massive comparisons of tale types or motifs that matched similar attempts by botanists, philologists, geologists, and biologists. Here again, we witness the absence of interest in particular tellers of tales. Context is stripped away in order to identify recurrent building blocks (motifs) of tales that might be found in various parts of the world over time, in both written and oral versions.

The basic system, since elaborated and refined, began as the project of Finnish folklorist Antti Aarne. Building on the work of his teachers, Julius Krohn and Krohn's son Kaarle, he developed a methodology by which to discover the historical and geographic origin and spread of tales. Aarne's student, Stith Thompson, continued Aarne's work; their *Aarne-Thompson Tale Type Index* (1961[1928]) and Thompson's subsequent six-volume *Motif-Index of Folk-Literature* (1960[1932–36]) became the best known, most widely consulted among collections of tales and their motifs, and they continue to be revised and supplemented, and also emulated. Hans-Jorg Uther in 2004 completed a three-volume revised edition.

Methodologically, when enough "similar" motifs (recurring characters, objects, actions or events) in a set of tales had been identified, those tales were considered variants of a given tale type. The type was assigned a number and given a title, which was often that of the best known variant. For example, tale-type 505 is the number for The Grateful Dead wherein a traveling hero sees to it that a corpse is buried and is later rewarded in some dramatic way by the grateful deceased person disguised as a fellow traveler (perhaps as an animal or angel). The tale type is listed first under "Fairy Tales" (300–750) and then under the subcategory "Supernatural Helpers," (500 to 559) in Aarne-Thompson-Uther (ATU). As is true for etic categories, tale types and motifs focus *first* on similarities—relating different tales and motifs to an overarching category the scholar constructs—before noting differences.

Motifs, basic building blocks of the tales, are categorized alphabetically A through Z. For example, Animal Motifs are listed under B and Deception Motifs under K. To discuss the magical thinking of Deadheads, Revell Carr identifies several well-known grateful dead motifs recurrent in their stories such as: A114.2.1 (deity born in shape of egg), D1825.7 (magic sight of incident before it happens), D1610.3.4 (speaking musical instrument), D2143.1.2 (rain produced by singing), N202 (wishes for good fortune realized).

While there are over 2,500 tale types, there are more than ten times that many motifs. These motifs are found in more than one tale, strung together in different ways, and most tales contain more than one. As Steven Swan-Jones put it, "motifs have a life of their own" (1995: 4) They are notoriously slippery to define or work with, but fascinating. Recently a group of European scholars (Darányi, Wittek, and Forró n.d.) have studied motifs as analogous to DNA strands and are developing computer programs that will illustrate how motifs slip among various tales and also how tellers use them differently in various tales (Darányi and László 2012).

Again, the impetus for fixing tale types was to compare and categorize similar tales—like dragon slayers, ATU 300, found in Japan, Ireland, Egypt, Estonia, among the Hittites, and so forth—through history and across geography. As the diffusion of culture groups over time and space was studied by tracing the spread of languages or material culture items, so folklorists traced the global diffusion of folk motifs and folktales. They theorized that geographically widespread tales could be traced back to a single version if enough oral and early written variants could be found, and that they spread most often by means of human contact and not by independent invention. Why were these efforts important? Carl Lindahl neatly sums up Thompson's goal for this method: "Behind Thompson's work stood a now long-discarded grand theory (*origin is essence*) and its inevitable corollary (*because origin is essence, we can and must discover it*) (2010: 259).

At first, these indices focused on tales of Europe and the Near East, but gradually lists of tales and motifs from other parts of the world have been added or built using the same or similar systems. The aim of earlier studies, including the pre—Aarne-Thompson study of Cinderella stories by Marian Cox in 1893, was to discover where and when written and oral variants had been found (Cox identified 345 variants from 80 countries), as well as the tale type's "original habitat" (Burne 1913: 435). The complete study of just one such tale would, as Lindahl writes, "be the defining work of the scholar of traditional narrative" (2010: 259). Yet, he adds, finding that first home proved "a scholarly fantasy" (259). As folklorist Andrew Lang somewhat meanly remarked in his introduction to Cox's book, *Cinderella*, all that could be safely predicated of *Cinderella's* origin was that the tale could not have arisen among a naked and shoeless people (Cox 1893).

From Similarities to Differences

American folklorist Rosemary Zumwalt recounts attacks on the historic-geographic system in the mid-twentieth century. She cites folklorist and ethnomusicologist Alan Lomax, who wonders deferentially but forthrightly, what the achievements of the method could be since origins were not discovered, and refers to it as "sterile" (qtd. in Zumwalt 1988: 110). Furthermore, she reports that although Thompson thought separation of the folk from the lore allowed a "more dispassionate reading of the material" (111), folklorists were beginning to insist on consideration of storytellers as both creators and interpreters. She quotes Albert Lord of *Singer of Tales* fame, "I wonder whether it is possible to arrive at any archetype of a tale or a song or an epic, if we consider that in every performance . . . the individual singer introduces variations" (qtd. in Zumwalt 1988: 111). Whether folklorists were literary or anthropological, they were (in the former case) moving away from their central interest in discovering "original tales," (in the latter) from discovering "original" cultures, and (in both cases) from tracing paths of diffusion.

Carl Lindahl writes that

> one kernel concept continued to thrive. The narrative indexes and tale-type studies developed by Thompson and others could *help us to document and compare narrative traditions and to discover the recoverable history, distribution, and changes in the tales.* We would see the tales change, noting *how* they change to fit the esthetics, values, and concerns of each group that shares them. (2010: 259)

Thus, Lindahl modifies and localizes the approach. Drawing on the Leonard Roberts' intense and focused study of the folktales in a small section of eastern Kentucky, Lindahl emphasizes how the "fingerprints" or records of similar stories from other places and times can illuminate what is new and different in a handed down tale. He turns our attention from similarities to differences: "The moment of performance is the instant of emergence, but it takes a profound knowledge of the fingerprint to comprehend from what, precisely, the performance is emerging" (2010: 260). Study of the present condition is now central, but while a story's past may be blurred by time, it can provide significant insight in terms of understanding how the contemporary aesthetic is deployed.

Today, folklorists continue to cite tale types and motifs in order to compare (and contrast) them. Imperfect as the system is, and perhaps that is part of its charm, every aspiring folklorist or fellow traveler should peruse the tale-type and motif indices. Most folklorists do attempt to note tale types or motifs in their publications, and often this lets the scholar step back to gain insight at a higher level of abstraction and avoid nationalist claims to lore ownership.

Particular, recent examples of historic-geographic studies that draw on motif and tale-type collections are studies by Jason Baird Jackson and by Russian folklorists Andrey Korotayev, Yuri Berezkin, the late Artem Kozmin, and Alexandra Arkhipova. Each focuses heavily on diffusion studies or global cultural flows of tales and their tellers. In each case, the scholars draw on tales and motifs with far-flung variants in order to criticize geographical hegemonies. In doing so, they employ comparative folklore documentation that challenges geographical and social grand narratives.

In the first of these, Jackson (2013) draws from the legend of Dido's founding of ancient Carthage. Around 800 BCE, Dido (Elissa), a royal Phoenician, fled to the western Mediterranean after her father, the king, died and her brother murdered her husband. In this particular tale (legend) Dido and her people ask the local inhabitants (Berbers or *Amazigh*) for only as much land as can be measured with one ox hide. As expected by those familiar with tale type AT 2400 (ATU 927c*) or motif K185.1, Dido tricks her hosts by cutting the hide in a long, thin, continuous strip that stretches enough to encircle a lovely hill looking out over the Mediterranean, thus establishing Carthage, a suburb of present-day Tunis.

The stories in Jackson's article, though, all take place in North America. Jackson draws on similar tales from many times and places to note commonalities and differences in ways colonialist incursions have been "managed." All in all, the stories are accounts of clever bartering during first encounters between unevenly matched duelists—newcomers and those established on the land. As Jackson illustrates, sometimes local inhabitants win and other times newcomers triumph. He quotes Sadhana Naithani, writing in 2004, "Colonialism generated space for many kinds of new oral discourses: the colonisers talking about the colonised (which is largely known and studied) and the colonised talking about the colonisers. The latter area of research remains almost untouched" (qtd. in Jackson 2013: 31). Indeed, the latter research now engages cultural anthropologists and folklorists. In the process they often scramble taken-for-granted hierarchies of scholarship by recovering the little known work of earlier folklore scholars who may have been listening to "the colonised talking about the colonisers" in coded ways.

Another interesting example of recentering is "Return of the White Raven: Postdiluvial Reconnaissance Motif A2234.1.1 Reconsidered" (2006) by Andrey Korotayev, et al. The authors take issue with an earlier monograph by Swedish folklorist Anna Birgitta Rooth (1967), in which she claims that the story of the white raven after the flood was spread to Native Americans by missionaries. They, rather, identify an Arabic interpretation of the story of Noah's ark, taken from the Pentateuch as the source for these stories.

MORE *DUST ON THE FOLKLORISTS?*

In 1980, as I was defending my dissertation, one of my committee members asked me a question that took me aback. It subtly but clearly accused me of copying from a book one of the North African personal experience narratives I had discussed in the dissertation. Why? Because, my interrogator said, the story was too good to have been orally recounted!

Naively or not, I was bemused and proud that the little town in North Africa where I had spent six years of my young adult life was the home of older men who could tell such good stories, and pleased that I had been able to share some of them. But why would a folklorist suspect that a story was too sophisticated to be an oral narrative? Had the little story (Reynolds 2007 104–7; Webber 1991: 102–8) about a deceased North African (who may have been a holy man), a young boy, and a hawk been too cleverly crafted to be the oral narrative of a semiliterate country man? Is the story too "classy," too subtle and multilayered—too "evolved," in other words?

Whether lore is judged by artistic or scientific standards, most disciplines are inclined to conclude that the so-called "simple forms," André Jolles' *einfache formen*, the oral, original, lore of the folk (myth, legend, fairy tale, and such) are, at best, on their way to a "higher" standard: Written literature is almost invariably perceived as farther up on the evolutionary scale than oral literature; mainstream, Western medicines are "better" than the folk medicine on which they are often based; folk music becomes "high art" when appropriated into a symphony.

Although we have, at least in most circles, left behind the notion of racial inferiority and social Darwinism, the division between literate and illiterate may have replaced it in these "postmodern" times. Emphasis on another "great divide" between the minds of oral communities and literate ones continued into the last half of the twentieth century. It seems we cannot escape comparing and finding ourselves superior to a "savage mind" that needs to be domesticated by the printed word. Political scientist and anthropologist James C. Scott (2009) has tied literacy to domination by the state and introduces in reference to the unlettered, the provocative term, at least for students of verbal art, "post-literate."

At the same time, an opposing academic discourse also closely tied to folkloristics claims that we have lost the best of our old stories—that they have devolved—or that we have lost knowledge that must be rediscovered. Comparing past and present in the context of root heritage may elevate the past. Current oral literatures in Greece or Egypt, for example, may be dismissed as inferior to their "pure" classical forebears. Implied in the question to Dr. Johnson about the Ossian epics (chapter 1) is the idea that we have lost the oral prowess we once had—in the time of Homer or in Biblical times or in ancient India.

This perspective, too, derives from the transfer of Darwinian biological theories to social theory. As an attractive species—a beautiful bird or a luminous fish—might be wiped out by a more viable but less attractive species, so the progress of civilization has endangered forms produced by the primitive mind. Or the devolution of oral narratives might have been caused by Müller's disease of language where, just as a species might weaken and fail, so might a narrative become enfeebled, falling from a noble myth in India to a "simple" folk tale in Europe.

A major dimension of folkloristic thought has been the understanding that change is not always for the better and that "evolving" doesn't imply improvement. We do respect past actors and events as being every bit as complex and multifaceted as those of the present. By dismissing the past as simpler than the present we colonize it and miss what we can learn from it. Yet, folklorists also tend to critique their own neglect of the new. Question: "How many folklorists does it take to change a light bulb?" Answer: "Three: One to change it and two to talk about how the old one was better."

STRUCTURALISM

The sort of analysis attempted here suggests . . . a study that can transcend a conception of structure either as simply equivalent to conscious rule or as necessarily unconscious and that can understand structure as sometimes emergent in action.

—Dell Hymes, "Breakthrough into Performance"

These words of well-known folklorist, anthropologist, linguist, and sociolinguist Dell Hymes are taken from the 1975 collection, *Folklore: Performance and Communication.* Hymes both sums up and implies a critique of structuralist practice, which was near its zenith at that time. As a linguistic anthropologist studying poetic speech, he looked to folkloristics to inject considerations of performance and the performer into the study of language. Two sorts of structuralism (along with related semiotic studies) permeated folklore and surrounding disciplines, especially anthropology and sociolinguistics, at that time. These were dominated by the approaches of Claude Lévi-Strauss' *Mythologiques I–IV* (Lévi-Strauss 1964, 1966, 1978, 1981) and Vladimir Propp's *Morphology of the Folktale* (2008). Folklorists focused particularly on Lévi-Strauss' approaches to myth and on Propp's to the folktale.

Structuralism is loosely defined as recognizing and foregrounding how elements of the cultural imaginary, often expressed or negotiated through expressive culture, must be understood as interrelated and interdependent pieces of a larger structure or system. This move led away from comparing small nuggets like dragon motifs (dragon fight to free princess, B 11.11.4; fire-breathing dragon, B11.2.11; human sacrifice to a dragon, B11.10) from around the world. Structuralists focused on how elements within a myth or tale must relate to one another to move the narrative forward and on how structures in stories related to social or cosmological understandings or logics. Further, a collection of narratives might have comparable structures.

During the first three quarters of the twentieth century, structuralism was a major theoretical approach for many disciplines. Over time, structuralist theories and methodologies with different emphases found particular favor among linguists, psychologists, anthropologists, literary critics, and folklorists. Specific variations of motifs and tale types were less foregrounded in any particular study of lore; rather, studies focused on an underlying structure ("discovered" or "uncovered" through various methods) that would allow researchers to generalize at a higher level of abstraction. Rather than comparing tale types or motifs from around the world, plucked from their local narrative or cultural contexts, scholars focused on the scientific importance of the conscious (Propp's folktales) or unconscious structure (Lévi-Strauss) underlying narratives grouped culturally.

Like Müller, Lévi-Strauss privileged myth as the way to understand basic human inclinations, and his approach was very much philological. He was not interested, for example, in privileging participant observation. Lévi-Strauss eschewed the study of any particular event. The focus on interpreting the structured collective unconscious of a group tended to foreclose any possibility of small group freedom or agency and thus any need for in-depth fieldwork. Despite Lévi-Strauss' reputation as an anthropologist, his approach to myths was philological, philosophical, and literary. He, too, plucked myths from their local and performative milieus and took control of their cultural contexts in his nonetheless compelling interpretations.

Lévi-Strauss sought an underlying structure of relationships that would be comparable across a set of myths that might vary in terms of their surface content; he intended to establish, finally, patterns of thought that are shared by all humankind. Although dubbed an anthropologist, he was introduced to anthropology by his first wife. He spent no more than six months in the field and closely resembled armchair anthropologists like Frazer. Ironically, Lévi-Strauss' ability to unpack Brazilian myths depended on how strange these myths remained to him in his failure to study their local cultural, social, or linguistic contexts.

Vladimir Propp, like Müller, was a philologist. In his famous study of the morphology of Russian folktales, Propp emphasized how certain motifs related to each other in a whole set of similar tales. His work was published in Russian in 1928 but didn't get much notice until it was translated into English thirty years later, just as Lévi-Strauss' works were gaining attention in the English-speaking world. For Propp, an identical or similar motif, if it showed up in a different part of a story, fulfilled a different "function" in that story plot. For Russian tales, he identified thirty-one ordered functions. Interdiction, function #2 (e.g., "don't speak"), or lack, function #8 (no magic potion), would be two examples. Contrast this kind of comparison with Lévi-Strauss' cacophony of mythemes (essential kernels of a myth), so that an old lady, shit, and a turtle all turn out to be interchangeable, as one of my fellow graduate students used to bemoan. And, each element's significance depends not only on how the turtle is characterized in such particular mythemes but even more on how that mytheme then interconnects with other mythemes syntagmatically (with the other words before and after it) within a particular myth. In both cases, the focus is on the narrative order or structure, rather than on certain motif or story ingredients.

Dell Hymes' seminal work, "Breakthrough into Performance" (1975) includes a comparative analysis of three Chinook (Native American) renderings of a particular part of a cycle of Coyote trickster tales. While he does not mention either Lévi-Strauss or Propp specifically, Hymes rebalances their approaches to the comparative study of oral narrative. Whether structure is "necessarily unconscious and across cultures" (Lévi-Strauss' myths) or, alternatively, "conscious rule" (Propp's Russian folktales), it needs to be studied with an awareness of differences that emerge in each performance. For all their differences, it became clear to Hymes and to many students of verbal art that structuralism as practiced by Lévi-Strauss and Propp lacked an important dimension, structure as "emergent in action." Only by witnessing the performance of a piece of verbal art can a student of a genre appreciate it as a distinctive realization of possibilities.

Structuralism, at least as Lévi-Strauss imagined it, allowed for the very rich unpacking of a text syntagmatically and paradigmatically. However, by ignoring individual performances and performers, this approach precluded attention both to the text's meaning to its own folk community and to how a narrative, *corrido* (Spanish for ballad), epic, or riddle might comment on the past, the present, and the future. Oddly, the historic and geographic were of little interest to structuralists, myth being considered both timeless and unattached to place. Rather, such studies were meant to uncover basic, universal patterns that structure all human consciousness.

COMPARING VERBAL ART AND MATERIAL CULTURE STRUCTURES

Folklore field studies began with the study of regional patterns and diverged toward an effort to discover general structures of human consciousness. Nevertheless, folklorists found ways to use structuralism that combine field research and the historical and cultural contexts of folk communities. The lore of wordsmiths and folk artists merged repeatedly with touchstones of structuralism: (1) binary oppositions considered basic to conceptualization of any subject, (2) emphasis on how systems function synchronically (currently) rather than diachronically (unfolding over time), and (3) the privileging of paradigms over syntagms. As I have indicated, structural studies tended to be tied to verbal arts and to linguistic models, but structures also formed the basis of studies of, for example, house or barn types.

These architectural types might be compared in order to identify how particular communities disbursed and intermingled—the kinds of home or barn styles people brought with them as they migrated from one region to another. In his book *Folk Housing in Middle Virginia* (1973), Henry Glassie adapted structuralist methods to the study of vernacular housing, not studying the diffusion of house types, but rather the sociohistorical contexts in which the housing "lived." Glassie "read" material culture, relying on material culture artifacts and their contexts and listening to inhabitants' stories, in the absence of historical records, to study social change over time.

An interesting study by Jeanette Harries, "Pattern and Choice in Berber Weaving and Poetry" (1973), uses both structuralist methodologies and close participant observation, allowing her theory to emerge from her data. This is a useful study, for it turns toward specific occasions of performance and focuses on process rather than product when comparing folk poetry and weaving. She asserts that among Tamazight-speaking Berbers (*Amazigh*) in central Morocco (and by implication in other societies as well) there is "a structural analogy between . . . [Berber poetry] genres and . . . weaving" (175).

The underlying structural processes of poetry and weaving are not foregrounded, as they are for Propp and Hymes. Rather, communally negotiated agreement about what composition should look like is the basis for the innovative, "performative" dimension of the process of weaving, whether of a poem or a carpet. The community assumes the structure will be constant and taken for granted (though open to renegotiation), while what is of interest is "individual talent and application" (175), or creativity, within these rubrics. This is an example of what might be called a sociostructural study—one that compares within rather than between communities; looks at process and not simply product in folk art; and brings into conversation shared understandings of structure among men and women and between verbal art and material culture. Harries demonstrates how communities share not only the structural means of building up a poem or carpet (the process) but also particular themes or motifs.

This increased attention to "agency, the current and more complex term for what used to be called the individual or personal element in anthropologies seeking to avoid structural overdetermination"

(Anderson 1997: 204) is accompanied by attention to underlying structures that may help ethnographers focus on a community's shared understanding of itself, its particular "social imaginary." This process remains a fruitful tool to organize intangible and affective data.

Interestingly, whereas Glassie, when he draws on the tools of structuralism to understand folk artifacts, finds that a universal principle of Western folk design is a repetitive and symmetrical aesthetic (Schlereth 1982: 125), Harries finds for the Berbers that in regard to symmetry, "Berber poetry and weaving differ from Western expectations" (1973: 179). There is no expectation of perfect symmetry in either medium, and she adds that, "weavers seem not to share my notion of symmetry" (185). This may have to do with the process of creating a communal poetry performance, which is emergent in terms of who is participating at any particular moment, how well they know each other, how skilled they are, whether both men and women are participating, and what the occasion is. A carpet, on the other hand, takes months to create on a loom that rolls the finished motifs back out of sight so rows may be balanced in size, but not in motif.

The field of semiotics has become useful to many folklorists and cultural/linguistic anthropologists with its emphasis on sign *systems* and its interest in underlying relations among elements within cultural domains or among genres. In some ways semiotics is more appealing than literary theory because it looks beyond the foregrounding of speech to an understanding of foodways, quilts, house types, and so forth on their own evaluative terms, rather than within a system dominated by literary texts. And, as in the example by Harries above, semiotics opens up a space for comparing underlying structures among or between not only genres, but media, whether materially or verbally expressive.

CONCLUSION

Nineteenth-century liberalism established a normative vision of what globalization should add up to: "nature's own plan" as "discovered"; "the (lettered, male, European) eye that held the system could familiarize ('naturalize') new sites/sights immediately upon contact, by incorporating them into the language of the system" (Pratt 1992: 31). Yet, comparativism has also been an important resource deployed by subordinated groups to (re)establish contexts and scales of relation, and identities, personas, and worldviews to claim stature and distinction on a global stage (cf. Kris Manjapra 2013: 5). Folklorists have variously responded to what Manjapra refers to as a "thickening of entanglements" and others call "collusion" to foreground the ways in which folk artists and their communities upset assumptions about the comparable values of communities around the globe and form alliances that scramble a Western meta-perspective of the world and its human resources.

In one way or another, folklorists draw on the historic-geographic methodologies, tale-type and motif indices, and structuralist strategies or combinations of these comparative practices to attend to questions of social, ethnic, regional, national, or other communal situatedness to provide much needed insight into the aesthetics of the human–communal condition.

Chapter Seven

Challenges for the Future
Folklore Today and Tomorrow

---

*We joined a profession that has charged us, like märchen heroes, with
an impossible task: to borrow, to study, to explain, to share, to preserve
an untranslatable immanence. We must understand and act upon the
understanding that traditions do not merely record or mirror lives but
can save lives as well.*

— Carl Lindahl, "Leonard Roberts, The Farmer-Lewis-Muncy Family,
and the Magic Circle of the Mountain Märchen"

A half century has gone by since Dundes and the other young Turks
rolled up their sleeves and (re)formed folkloristics. Part of that reformation
was rather a (de)formation that came about through the increasing inclu-
sivity of the discipline. The studied became the studier, or, at least, the
lines between informant and researcher were increasingly blurred. Women
scholars began to have an easier time, as did BGLTQ folklorists and people
of color. Those in disadvantaged circumstances, once marginalized in the
presentation and management of their own folklore in the exoteric "marketplace" of ideas, have gained agency. What is studied as folklore and how
folklore is studied (including self-critiques of ethnographic work and scholarly presentation, and consideration of the danger of blowback on individuals and communities) have become central issues in folkloristics.

Many folklorists now work (or come from) outside Western Europe
and North America. Attention to the performative "voices" of folk predomi-
nates over performative voices of folklorists. Perhaps most fruitfully, the
wedges marking off one discipline from another and separating "professionals" from "others" are more malleable. This pliability has been facilitated
by the rise of new media, a trend brought to general notice with Dundes'
attention to the office lore of middle-class, white-collar folk communities.

This final chapter offers several approaches to folklore studies
that, although not new, have been foregrounded recently as folklorists

have increasingly focused on new media and turned their attention to powerful theoretical insights and methodological practices found among a family of disciplines, unbound and reunited—bringing to light the relevance of social justice issues to folkloristics and vice-versa. Folkloristics has been enabled, too, by scholars' increased inclination to consider change or adaptation in performed lore not as debasing but rather as the very element that keeps aesthetic communicative practices relevant to present circumstances. Most of the topics below have been touched on, but in this final chapter we will revisit them and look ahead.

FOLKLORE AS CULTURAL COMMENTARY: THE AFFECTING PRESENCE

Folklore is not just another pretty (romantic) face, as some academic folk have dismissed it, and as many "public" folk within government or other political entities might wish it were. Rather, folklore as aesthetically fashioned culture rewards the sustained and intense study that is central to understanding cultural affect—the centripetal force that helps communities coalesce even in the face of poverty, war, plague, persecution, colonial hegemony, or famine. Paraphrasing Lindahl's (2010) words, folklore does not simply reflect creatively what is, but it creatively interrogates the status quo. As the locus of group or communal poetics, of artfully compressed culture, lore can be a powerful tool to "save lives" or ruin them.

Attention to folklore has much to offer the family of disciplines. Fabian writes in *Out of Our Minds* (2000) that what is often missing from ethnographic writing is a consideration of artistic or affective behavior necessary to understanding cultural life. Arriving at such insights requires a set of theoretical tools and strategies to unpack, analyze into its component elements, communally negotiated performances in order to understand why such aesthetically informed behavior is so powerful.

DISCIPLINARY TIGHT CHEMISES (AND LEADEN COWLS): FOLKLORE AND THE DISCIPLINES

But what I knew about Negro folklore was fitting me like a tight chemise. I couldn't see it for wearing it. It was only when I was off in college . . . that I could see myself like somebody else and stand off and look at my garment. Then I had to have the spy-glass of Anthropology to look through at that.

— Zora Neale Hurston, *Mules and Men*

As we have seen, among the consequences of modernity were the tight chemises of scientism, the privileging of divisions among disciplines, and the reification of professionalization. Now, we consider further the effects of the "tight chemises" of our own academic specializations, and the advantages of loosening them.

In her already classic "Fieldwork in Common Places" (1986), Mary Louise Pratt considers the blinkers ethnographers don when they define their work as "professional scientific work" (Malinowski 1948) and set themselves apart from other writers and visitors to the "other," whether missionaries, explorers, journalists, or colonial settlers. Pratt points out that these "professionals" seem(ed) unaware that they shared narrative tropes with other travel writers. Ethnographers' arrival narratives (their accounts of first encounters with "natives") are remarkably similar not only to one another but to accounts written by so-called amateur travelers whose works Malinowski dismissed as having been "killed by science."

The record of the traveler's first encounter with the "native(s)" must be compelling, because it represents the chronicler's first encounter with us readers and must draw us in to gaze with him or her at these "others." However, this encounter also reveals the writer's (romantic) gaze. I play with this trope in *Romancing the Real* (1991)—detailing the anticipation I feel each time I return to the field, acknowledging the betwixt and between sentimental attachment I am sharing with my readers, my quite *un*critical nostalgia. One would think that for an ethnographer, at least, attention might better be drawn to the inhabitants' first impressions of these strangers showing up on their literal or metaphorical doorsteps.

Pratt's "arrival" example is a succinct and powerful reminder of two contemporary focuses in studying expressive culture. First, whose points of view are we, as folklorists, trying to bring into conversation and understand? Second, how does adhering to reified and artificially sundered categories and dichotomies interfere with refining those understandings? By separating science from humanities or humanities from art, and making crabbed distinctions between disciplines, we miss important conversations about the practice of ethnography and ethnographic writing and about how oral, written, visual, and tactile media intertwine.

EVERYDAY FORMS OF RESISTANCE

Folklorists should be involved in the international political and social discourse more than we currently are, for we are one of the few fields (anthropology is another) especially ready to comment on the culturally constructed dimensions of political contexts, along with their rich complexities and ambiguities.

— Barre Toelken, "The End of Folklore"

Toelken's observation underscores the importance of the part folklore plays in social and political realms, not only in discourse, but in its many resources for presentation of self, for example, in the context of the *passeggiata*, as discussed in chapter 3. Folklore may resist in ways that most folklorists rarely want to consider; there is "mean girls" folklore, as well as classist, racist, and sexist folklore. This, too, must be studied more than it is. In my first folklore seminar, with folklorist Ellen Stekert at Berkeley in the 1970s, she told of recording an informant whose jokes she found repellant. She confided that she felt awkward encouraging him with her laughter, but she also felt the importance of understanding all variations of folklore and how and why individuals or groups engage it.

Stephen Gencarella writes in "Constituting Folklore" (2009) that "folklore . . . is something that in its doing, composes a folk, as both an immediate audience and a political category. Further, that doing constitutes antagonists or enemies to that folk—a people to kill and a people to kill for" (173). This certainly is true and part of folk wisdom. Some of my Somali students tell me that their parents refuse to teach them their tribal legends for fear of passing along violent rifts with Somalis of other tribes.

Sometimes, folklore constructs a middle ground. As counterhegemonic discourse, it can create a persuasive (imaginary?) space for people to resist and still win attention and appreciation from their opponents. Well-wielded lore can create a safer public space for individual voices as we learn from Dick Gregory (1964). "Poetically," the "others," if their "discourse" is clever enough, find agency and common ground with folks who would otherwise reject them. Scholars in their own tight chemises, intent on being scientific in their study of revolutions, can indeed overlook the power of affecting resistance. Unfortunately, but inevitably, the aesthetic or affective dimension of the crafted culture sometimes causes folklore to be overlooked as crucial social and political commentary. It is not a "sideshow."

FOLK AS CULTURAL COMMENTATORS: AGENCY

"The 'folk' are striking back," wrote Yiorgos Anagnostu in a 2006 article. "Historically the [laypeople], objects of representation by dominant classes and those who served their interests (colonial administrators, missionaries, travelers, intellectuals, and academic nation-builders, including folklorists and anthropologists) . . . are in the process of controlling their self-representation" (381). He later adds, "Operating outside the proper boundaries of the academy, folklore's popular bandits . . . deploy [their own] politics of . . . representation" (395).

As we saw in chapter 4, folk agency is facilitated as well by folklorists' and other ethnographers' increased awareness of how to collaborate with folk communities and performers, and a more subtle understanding of what a folk group might be. Folklorists are becoming more alert to the fact that we, from a wholly or partly exoteric perspective, may be making facile assumptions about what a folk community is and the process through which it is constituted. Gencarella proposes that "we treat folklore as a rhetorical act of instituting a people" (2009: 174). This gets at the crux. Who is instituting people—insiders or outsiders? I suggest that outsiders sometimes institute people with much broader sweeps of the rhetorical pen than the folk group itself—and institute groups based on etically foregrounded groupness categories—such as color, religion, gender, political stances). What follows are three examples of ways the "folk are striking back" with the collaboration of folklorists.

DOUBLE VISION: FOLKLORE DEPLOYED

When we went back into the [New Orleans Super] Dome, that was covered with trash, excrement and dead bodies, [the National Guard] made us all lie on the floor face down like criminals. They threw bedding, MRE's [ready to eat meals], water—and then left us there.

> — Ruby, Katrina survivor recorded by San Antonio resident and Ruby's host Judi Rice (qtd. in Carl Lindahl's "Legends of Hurricane Katrina")

Tuesday, 11 March, 2003, Baghdad Riverbend: Salam, . . . did you use the X pattern or the traditional "*"? Salam: The* star is good, but with particularly big windows I have been using a + and Xs in each quadrant.

> — Riverbend, a female Iraqi blogger, preparing for the U.S. bombs, blogging with Salam Pax

In 1954 a hydrogen bomb (code name Bravo), 750 times larger than the Hiroshima bomb, was tested in the Marshall Islands. It was detonated despite warnings of strong winds blowing towards inhabited islands. Great clouds of gritty ash rained down.

> — Jane Goodall, "Marshall Islanders' Painful Memories of Nuclear Testing"

Much conversation in folkloristics today has centered on strategies for listening and, in some scenarios, making room for "subalterns" to speak, to have a voice, to be heard by outsiders through their expressive culture in ways that will improve their circumstances. "Double vision"—or "counterethnography"—is a way to interweave divergent discourses by attending to media and genres that individuals find familiar, accessible, and (sometimes) safe. David Hanlon describes these collusive responses as ones that seek to know "in order to cope; and that in playful subversive ways reflect colonial anthropology back on itself" (qtd. in Buschmann 2009: 118). Examples from the period of colonization in the Pacific include local museums dedicated to artifacts of the colonizers (hence the term "double vision") or arrival stories told not by travelers but by their "hosts."

As a way to comprehend counterethnography, let us refer back to arrival-scene tropes. Let's look at three arrival scenes—one from the mid-twentieth-century and two from the early twenty-first—from the perspective of lesser-heard-from residents who fashioned creative responses to their uninvited "guests" in a variety of media and genres. The precipitous arrival scenes look quite different when viewed from the perspectives of, say, the Enewetak and Bikini Atolls of the northern Marshall Islands, 1946–1958; the inhabitants of Baghdad, 2003; and New Orleans, 2005. In two cases, the arrival scene features bombs, and in the third, a "natural" disaster resulting from a catastrophic engineering failure. Marshallese, Baghdadi, and New Orleansian groups have been displaced, many forever, from their extended families and communities and they can draw on affective discourse to say something about that.

How do these folk move themselves from periphery to center, victim to agent, in a world where many have lost their local communities and the incomers have more media time, louder voices, bigger bombs, and the ability to win contracts to build unreliable levees? How can communal expressive culture work when the community itself is destroyed? The introductory pages of Susan Slyomovics' *The Object of Memory*, are instructive. She reviews means by which lost communities of the last century in Jewish East Europe, Palestine, and Muslim Bosnia and Armenia are taking control of their own narratives of "traumatic loss of place." Her examples revolve around the folk communities' creation of memorial books, "active remembrance . . . as a guarantee of cultural survival" (xiv) and as pushback against the labels of victim or villain. The three following groups work toward similar goals.

Marshallese Trickster Tales

Philip McArthur writes of the Marshallese, "The islanders of the targeted atolls were not only forced to leave their homelands where myth, history, genealogy, and identity are inscribed into the landscape" (2008: 264), but many were abandoned on uninhabited islands to face near starvation, and thousands were exposed to nuclear fallout. Many not only contracted radiation poisoning but were then subjected to experiments on the effects of that poisoning. The death, suffering, and displacement ratios for Iraqis and New Orleansians are similarly shocking. One means of uniting a community is remembrance of a shared past. Most Marshall Islanders (http://mistories.org/intro.php) are now Christian, but in folklorist Philip McArthur's study of the Islanders' reaction to their treatment by the United States, notably to the testing of nuclear devices in/on their islands, the stories he was told were not contemporary, accusatory narratives but featured a figure from an earlier religion, the trickster god, Letao. Some Marshallese might prefer that overtly bitter tales of their oppression be told to outsiders rather than the trickster tales told to McArthur by Marshallese friends. But tale-tellers must judge the audiences they wish to reach—what stories will listeners near and far best be persuaded by?

Stories like Br'er Rabbit and the tales of Letao also have bitterness to convey, albeit with extreme complexity. Letting Letao take the stage opens up new perspectives on a collusive, multivalenced relationship linking the U.S. with Letao's trickiness and bad behavior. At the same time, continued U.S. dominance seems to be linked in multiple ways to Letao's continued willingness to lend the U.S. his magical, no-holds-barred attributes, or indeed to take responsibility for the damage done. I wouldn't be surprised if the assurance that letting the U.S. move inhabitants off their island homes in order to carry out nuclear tests would save the world from future wars doesn't rank among Letao's biggest lies. This "ownership" of both U.S. power and perfidy is different from and more sophisticated than what McArthur is told outside the performance frame. The Marshallese trickster-protagonists trouble local–global and U.S.–Marshallese dichotomies, as well as the military-industrial complex and its fallout.

Salam Pax: Gallows Humor

Groups experiencing violent incursion and displacement respond in a variety of ways. For Salam, managing the disasters involved a trickster-like blog that sought to gather together his former community, build a new one, and conceal his identity from his family, who did not know he was gay, and from his "evil boss unit." And he would keep out of reach of his government and the invaders (and journalists) who wanted to find him. His method was conversational and his primary genre was gallows humor.

During the lead-up to the Iraq war of March, 2003, Salam became a folk figure, "the most famous and most mysterious blogger in the world" (Peter Maas, *slate.com*). The exchange in the quotation above, between Salam and Riverbend, was written about a week before the March 19 U.S. invasion of Iraq and is about the aesthetic and practical aspects of the customary practice of duct-taping windows to avoid flying glass when bombs fall. Later we find that Salam hopes the curtains will be shredded by flying glass, as he thinks they are "hideous" and should be replaced.

Gallows humor is simply laughing in the face of death, or before terrifying or disastrous situations—including the invasion and consequent crime, disease, death, and displacement. A well-known example is Oscar Wilde's supposed deathbed gasp, playing on his own experience of gay stereotypes and his gay community, "either that wallpaper goes or I do." Salam, who wants to be prepared, includes "alcohol (red wine?) along with candles, good books and "crunchy munchies" in his list of what to stock up on. "I think that will get me through the bombing quite nicely," he blogs (2003: 1). Later that month he addresses his friend Raed, who is in Jordan studying and planning his marriage: "Raed . . . don't get married—come here and let's get bombed" (6).

A small joke like this can be interpreted in terms of its effect on audience(s) and what it does for the joker. Socially, as time went by, the blog drew on the poetics of a certain kind of humorous performance to keep the old community together, share that community with his readers, show a marked disdain for violence and oppression, and avoid the victim label. It could be said that such joking is a safety valve to help relieve stress, build morale, and bring confusion to the oppressors, but the value of creative speech lies in its ability to convey simultaneously multiple artistically informed messages that resonate differently for different individuals and audiences.

Referring back to Walters' (1999) article on Hurston, Salam's trickster self is "starting some shit" as part of a community renegotiating their own situation—both actually and metaphorically. More direct (unmediated) focus on audience members is also possible in the blog format. Audience members of Salam's folk community help foreground artistry in the performance, and their responses help negotiate reality. They may misinterpret, creatively resist, or simply ignore the subject positioning promoted by the author (Berger and Del Negro 2002: 67), or, or course, they also send validating messages or links.

Surviving Katrina

The work Texas public folklorist Pat Jasper and University of Houston folklorist Carl Lindahl are doing along with Katrina survivors and their hosts opens up space for a similar sort of conversation and, potentially, of agency. Their work connects survivors across space and time through the use of multiple media—radio programs, online programs, exhibits, and so on. In fact, the effectiveness of public folklore these days often comes from taking advantage of communicative modes rarely employed in the academy. Jasper's and Lindahl's efforts, in which the ivory tower and public folklore collaborate, can reflect on the effect their teaming up with traumatized citizens has on those citizens.

The project involves sharing stories told by survivors, to survivors, on the survivors' own terms. Crafting their own stories by drawing on the resources of folk culture could shape their futures, while, to the opposite effect, dominant voices in the media were depicting the survivors and the lost as criminals or, at best, helpless victims. In his article "Legends of Hurricane Katrina" (2012), Lindahl expresses his and Jasper's frustration at "blaming the victims" and dehumanizing the survivors. They opened space for what he calls "intimate strangers" to connect to counter the power of the media's powerful "legends," which tended to propagate stereotypes in which survivors were looked down on, literally and figuratively. In this way, survivors used their personal resources to "recreate their vanished communities and to forge new ones" (2012: 152).

Furthermore, they were able to break through three frames: the old scholarly frame that is skeptical of lay beliefs, the media frame that elevates negative rumors to the status of truths, and the "just–world" frame that posits the world is just and people get what they deserve and encourages the interviewer to blame the victim. These frames, Lindahl writes, have kept such stories off the record in the past. In Houston and San Antonio, people who had taken in survivors "formerly secure in the visual evidence projected from their TV sets were now watching those same TVs in the company of the survivors who had recently been pictured on the screens. Instance after instance, the news lost its purchase on truth" (Lindahl 2012: 140).

Similarly poignant reproaches have been produced by outsiders: to the bombs dropped on Baghdad ("Blind into Baghdad" (2004) by James Fallows) and about the atolls (see the film *Half-Life: A Parable for the Nuclear Age*, by the Australian, Dennis O'Rourke). In each case, the point of view we seek is that of those who, in one way or another, have been invaded. For folklorists, the stories survivors tell are not only tales of individual death and destruction but an unanticipated and violent rending of the social fabric of entire communities by forces set in play decades before and far outside their control.

In a forty-two-page letter to Dr. William F. Marcuson, III, then president of the American Society of Civil Engineers, UC Berkeley Professor Raymond B. Seed "allegorically" battles for "the soul of the profession" in the aftermath of engineering failures responsible for the scope of the post-Katrina disaster in New Orleans (http://www.lasce.org/documents/RaySeedsLetter.pdf). Seed reminds Marcuson that one of the first things professors teach engineering students is the difference between doctors and engineers: Irresponsible doctors kill patients one by one, but irresponsible engineers can and have killed people by the thousands.

Concluding, Seed dubs his letter a "saga," a term like "soul," and an allegory that reminds Marcuson of the consequences his science can have on human spirits. How do communities draw on communal expressive culture and customary practices to cope? Unitary responses to large-scale catastrophes don't exist, but folklore, as counterhegemonic and affecting discourse, can embolden us to "read against the grain," to subvert hierarchies. Like Letao, critical thinkers like Seed also can craft imaginaries that challenge local/global or engineer/humanist dichotomies.

AGENCY AND NEW MEDIA

The phonograph as a force in popular culture accelerated the process of corruption and decay of traditional ways of life—or so claimed many ethnographers.
— Erika Brady, *A Spiral Way*

It is easy to list reasons why technologies are not helpful to conventional ways of life. We think of people attached to their smartphones and their iPods, rather than sharing time playing musical instruments on the iconic front porch or exchanging tall tales or local history. Technologies, including both video and audio recordings, can aid in making local lore—dance music, or epics—vulnerable to appropriation, capture, or exploitation by nations or industries. "Digitization efforts dislodge texts and practices from . . . contexts, making it impossible to maintain epistemological holism and coherence" (Fish 2014: 17). Copyrighted or patented, some lore is frozen and homogenized while other forms are silenced. Still, it is striking that Erika Brady's *A Spiral Way* (1999) or Elizabeth Eisenstein's *The Printing Press as an Agent of Change* (1979) inspire a kind of critical nostalgia for older technologies similar to nostalgia for that communal front porch. The "flip side" is that, today, the movement toward increased agency, opening spaces for the voices of folk performers and the communities to which they belong, can be facilitated by more access to new and customary media.

As Alexander McDougal-Webber observes regarding the participation of youth in the Tunisian revolution (personal communication), youth spoke more boldly and with less fear once they extended their community by sharing artful performances of local, on-the-ground resistance (marches, music, chants, flash mobs) through blogs and YouTube documents. When they managed, unlike their parents' generation, to communicate around highly controlled conventional Tunisian media and tourist brochures, they captured the attention of sympathetic international television, radio, and newspaper audiences.

Creative people from within folk communities across the world can now be heard relatively unmediated, and new folk groups can emerge and take greater control of their messages and form/discover their own communities. Salam Pax's folk community is unmarked by any rounding up of "the usual suspects" we use to label a folk group: religious, occupational, gender, and so on. Can anyone but (or even) members of a folk community define that emergent and unstable entity? Folklorists are challenged to recognize the fluidity and ephemerality of groups, and how groups perceive their own coherence at any particular moment. An amalgam of new and conventional media data could also help us better understand the dynamics of our own or other folk groups.

Much as Giselinde Kiupers (2006) describes Internet disaster jokes regarding 9/11 as instances of playing with genres, so Salam's blog is a pastiche of generic conventions "borrowed from the news media, the entertainment industry, and popular culture" (qtd. in Hathaway 2005: 52) and more. At one point, he reminds the invaders to bring copies of *Democracy for Dummies*. More direct (unmediated) focus on audience members is made possible in the blog format as well. The audience members help foreground artistry in the performance, and their input and responses help negotiate reality. Thus, vernacular creativity is disbursed. As Noyes points out in "Group" (1995), there are multiple ways to belong to a folk community, and individuals within the community find what works for them.

In a book on folkloristics by Robert A. Georges and Michael Owen Jones (1995), we read that "people everywhere learn most of their folklore directly from those with whom they interact regularly and most intimately, thus requiring no movement or migration for folklore to be diffused through time and space" (144–145). "Interact regularly" has taken on new meaning in these times of social media, so that those with whom one interacts daily, if not hourly, may constitute a folk community despite other differences. Folklorist Dan Ben-Amos' (1971) well-known definition of folklore as artistic communication in small groups now encompasses groups that can include both next door neighbors and people who are continents away.

PUBLIC FOLKLORE: BETWEEN "LOOKY-LOOS" AND THE CLASH OF CIVILIZATIONS

You start out playing for people who are just like you. That's the only place you can. You play for people who come from where you come from. They . . . understand what you're doing, so you feel like you're

doing it for them. . . . Then one day, you're not playing for people like
you anymore.
— Waylon Jennings to Dave Hickey, "Romancing the Looky-Loos"

A public folklorist is the go-between who helps audiences outside
the folk community be more than what Waylon Jennings refers to as
"looky-loos." Jennings misses playing in a community, to an audience,
that understands where he is coming from and lets him know when he
goes wrong. Like Jennings' musical reach, once Salam's "fan base" got
too big, he also ended up with an audience of people who do not "recognize" him in all his betwixt and betweenness.

A folklorist in such circumstances can be a mediator and over
time even adopted into the community for which s/he wishes to be an
interpreter. Public folklorists in particular seek to unpack for outsiders the communal expressive culture of particular folk groups or the
personalities within them in ways that reconnect for outsiders the folk
on their own terms with their lore. They humanize for potential looky-
loos the communities or individuals who produce or hone a body of lore,
reattaching it and perhaps decommodifying it.

In the introduction to their book, *Public Folklore* (2007), Robert
Baron and Nicholas Spitzer write that the field of public folklore "is . . .
collaborative and dialogical, involving folklore applied . . . or presented
in new contexts *within and beyond* the communities where it origi-
nates" (viii; emphasis mine). Contrasting with efforts like UNESCO's
struggles to protect folkways worldwide, most public folklorists can
turn their attention to particular folk communities and specific projects. Work can be "highly local" and draw on methodologies that can
vary depending on particular settings.

Public folklorists are also often affiliated with universities. Barry
Gewen, in a 2008 *New York Times* piece, writes that public intellectuals
"might be journalists or academics, but only because they had to eat. . . .
Ideas for them were not building blocks to a career. Rather, careers were
the material foundation that allowed them to define and express their
ideas." This might describe public folklorists as well, always in the field,
always in public. Yet, unlike public intellectuals as Gewen describes them,
public folklorists, doubtless due to their embrace of communal performance
and their intense dialogue with folk communities, are not necessarily recognized through literary output. Rather, for folk communities and their
traditions to be accessible to diverse audiences, public folklorists need to
master not only folkloristics but also multiple media—new and old. They
need to report back, "through signage, commentary, design, editorial and
other devices in print, broadcast or exhibition and film production, and
through spoken introductions and colloquies with performers" (Baron and
Spitzer 2007: ix). Scholarly understanding is only the beginning.

Their role requires a wide range of expertise, and only extroverted folklore scholars with boundless energy and creativity, as well as the usual scholarship, need apply. It is also a delicate negotiation. In the words of Richard Kurin, both "collaboration with the people whose culture is being represented . . . [and] . . . the protocols of the community that is custodian of a certain folk heritage need to be observed" (2004: 1). Like all folklore fieldwork, the ideal is "an exchange of knowledge and skills which [sic] empower both parties and encourage cross-cultural understanding and continuing meaningful exchanges" (1). The ethical stakes are high.

In their betwixt and between role, public folklorists work against the insidiously self-fulfilling idea of a "clash of civilizations," the belief that some cultures and religions are so different from others that they can never be reconciled. Well-known political scientist Samuel Huntington (2004) has written about the West versus Islam and China, and about the deleterious effects of Hispanic civilization on U.S. culture. This unfortunate stance harks back to the culture-clash ideas of the colonial period, and is the antithesis of attempts Kurin outlines above to open a space where folk groups may achieve an appreciation of the "other" by making familiar what at first might be strange, and consequently gaining new insights into their own folk-ways by making the familiar strange, challenging our own folk groups to take a second look at beliefs and practices we take for granted.

Public folklorists also tend to projects that, although they may have profound global implications, take a different approach to community sustainability. More and more, "scholar activists" work at the intersections of folklore and economic and environmental realities. The urgency of this work emerges from studies at a local level that expose the vulnerabilities of those locals, whether urban, rural, or suburban communities. Michael Luster and Rachel Reynolds Luster, working with folklore and heritage studies at the University of Arkansas, are engaging "the strain within our field, which is devoted neither entirely to academic study nor to publicly funded public displays of traditional life, but rather to the sustaining of tradition *in situ* as a vital part of healthy and enduring community life" (http://www.afsnet.org/resource/resmgr/Best_Practices_Reports/Luster_Cultural_Sustainabili.pdf).

Their goal resonates with the work of folklorist Mary Hufford, including her study of forests of the Central Appalachian plateaus. The goal, and we will see other examples of this, is to take into account how inhabitants of a "globally significant resource" (Hufford et al. 2007: ii) have participated over time in cultural conservation practices so that drawing on their collective memories would be imperative in efforts to regenerate and protect the forest and watershed. Local stud-ies that interweave all dimensions of place—cultural practices inter-twined with a harmonious relationship with the landscape and its flora and fauna—can, Hufford persuades, ameliorate "the effects of global climate change" (Hufford et al. 2007: iv).

SOCIAL JUSTICE AND HERITAGE PROTECTION IN A GLOBAL SETTING

In the absence of local knowledge, global judges depend on wisdom.
— Dorothy Noyes, "The Judgment of Solomon"

Although "studying up" has been an overt focus of folkloristics at least since the mid-twentieth century (Nader, 1974[1969]), folklorists have had a fascination, if not always empathy, for seemingly vulnerable folk—the poor, the colonized, workers, children, women, rural people, migrants, and people with lifestyles that by choice or by chance make them "other." A book remains to be written addressing all the reasons for fascination with these "others," although some of them we have addressed earlier: resistance to loss (of languages, arts, heritage); the search for origins; fascination with perceived earthiness, whether gentle (Hawaii, Tahiti, Eden) or fierce (cannibals); the search for a better—or deliciously evil—way of being.

Customs and practices, from folk art to folk medicine to music to foodways, have been appropriated without attribution. Sometimes folk communities are romanticized and commodified while being driven out of existence. As a fisherman said to folklorist Kelly Feltault as she was interviewing him for a preservation and tourism project in the mid-Atlantic United States, "How are you going to preserve my culture if you don't save my right and ability to fish?" (2006: 90). In North Africa when I hear "save the Medina" I find that may mean livening up old facades, putting up historical plaques, and selectively nudging out businesses and inhabitants to "save" the Medina for academics and tourists.

Various entities (folklorists, indigenous peoples, nations) are attempting legal solutions to protect inherited expressive practices. How to protect the rights (various sorts of *changing* expressivity and knowledge) of communities, or the communities themselves, concerns folklorists, but these issues are also, as Noyes notes above, receiving a good deal of attention from organizations focused on intellectual property rights that generalize well beyond any particular local. Specific nations and their specialists are involved, as well as international agencies–like the ICH (Intangible Cultural Heritage), which is part of UNICEF and now has over 150 members (the United States is not a member) (http://www.unesco.org/culture/ich/index.php?lg=en&pg=00006).

TRICKY LAWS

In an article in the *American Indian Law Review* in 1998, "Frozen Rights in Canada: Constitutional Interpretation and the Trickster," John Borrows discusses cases addressing the Canadian constitution, which specifically guarantees Aboriginal and treaty rights in order "to shield collective Aboriginal rights from erosion due to [the Canadian Charter of Rights and Freedom's] individualist orientation" (37). Borrows considers a situation wherein the Supreme Court of Canada rules against the Canadian Indian rights to "harvest and sell resources within their territories" or to allow gaming within those territories. Thus, Borrows argues, the court undermines "the future commercial competitiveness and survival of Aboriginal nations in contemporary Canadian society" (39).

Borrows, a professor of law at the University of Minnesota and a member of Ontario's Chippewas of Nawash First Nation and Anishinaabe, draws on indigenous traditions, especially the collective wisdom of native tricksters, to challenge the narrow understanding of what "tradition" means and the consequences of that (mis)understanding. Borrows instructs, "First Nations have an intellectual tradition that teaches about ideas and principles that are partial and incomplete . . . through a character known as the trickster" (1998: 39). He explains that the "trickster's interaction with the court is an effective vehicle for examining law because: 'Stories are a great device for probing the dominant narrative. We use them to examine the presupposition, the body of received wisdoms that pass as truth but actually are contingent, power-serving, and drastically disadvantage our people'" (40 and quoting Richard Delgado).

Reminiscent of the Marshallese Letao, the trickster generates "a language between 'western' and 'aboriginal' accounts of law" (Borrows 1998: 41), and the trickster might be either a member or critic of the court. In this betwixt and between way he can talk back to and expose the "hidden cultural (dis)order" (41) of the legal argument. For, the "nine people . . . dressed in red, with white ermine framing their . . . traditional regalia" (42) have clearly assumed their trickster roles as well.

The majority decision in this case was that Aboriginal people's rights only extend to those traditions extant when Europeans appeared on the scene. To prevail, claimants would have had to "demonstrate that the practice, tradition or custom *was* a central and significant part of the society's distinctive culture" (Borrows 1998: 48; emphasis added). Borrows recognizes that change, by definition, is as much a part of tradition, if not more so, than stasis. Tricky courts can still make decisions based on an idea of supposed past purity and, unlike the trickster, deny the (always) hybrid. Two dissenting justices recognized this. One referred to the precontact rule as inappropriately crystallizing rights "at an arbitrary date" (Borrows 1998: 49) and another wrote that, by this rule's "logic," Aboriginal societies are denied "the right to adapt, as all peoples must, to the changes in the society in which they live" (50). Borrows wonders (trickily): "What would it be like for European-Canadians to have their fundamental rights defined by what *was* integral to European people's distinctive culture prior to their arrival in North America?" (54). Certainly, 200–300 years ago many European-Canadians were routinely disadvantaged on the basis of sex, class, or race. Today, he concludes, Aboriginals should be able to sell computers as well as moccasins.

YOGA AND RICE

Some thirty years ago, a student of mine, married to a Saudi Arabian, brought me, in Columbus, Ohio, a house-warming gift of an enormous bag of rice that she had brought from Saudi. I took some with me when I visited former Peace Corps friends living in Berkeley. The brother of one friend enthused, "*Where* did you get this rice?" It seems he had been in the Peace Corps in India in the 1960s and never could find in the U. S. the equal of the rice he had enjoyed there.

In 1997, the United States Patent Office allowed Ricetec, a company based in Texas (owned by a Liechtenstein prince), to file for some 20 patents to develop unique variants of basmati, long assumed to be part of the indigenous plant wealth of the Punjab region of India and Pakistan. After antiglobalization protests for which basmati was a "poster child," Ricetec withdrew 15 claims early in this century (Irai 2001). In a digital age, local forms and expressions are more and more (easily) appropriated by individuals, private companies, and public entities (or combinations thereof) to be managed and marketed. Often what is to be sold is not simply a practical item or practice, but "exotic" expressive culture as well. As scholar Allison Fish observes (personal communication), "It is the fact that these foreign jurisdictions are permitting the patenting of South Asian cultural heritage that makes Indian officials upset." There is an affective dimension to such communal heritage that makes the "piracy" crueler, more like theft of a local identity than simple threat of commercial loss, as significant as that, too, might be. (Notice that such claims of "origin," of geographical indications [GI of source," are similar to those for labeling only sparkling wine produced in the Champagne region of France "Champagne.")

Heritage pilfering can be fought in world courts if it can be proved that the product or practice has been in use for centuries as medicine, as sustenance, or as integral elements of religious ceremonies. Ignoring contributions of local communities in developing products and not allowing them to share the profits can be actionable (Fish 2014). We have seen similar issues with the pirating of music (Sunder 2012). As we saw earlier, material culture items are susceptible to appropriation, as they are so easily commodified, but intangible heritage is also vulnerable, especially in the digital age.

In response to these issues, India has set up a Traditional Knowledge Digital Library (TKDL) to rectify problems with global patent systems that allow cultural piracy—in the case of South Asia of turmeric or basmati—but also to resist attempts to patent certain practices of yoga. The rare, exotic, or "authentic" are particularly in play with traveling practices as teachers of from South Asia (for yoga), from the Arab world (for "belly dancing"), and from South America (for Salsa) are perceived as the embodiment of the art (Bock and Borland 2011, Fish 2014). Allison Fish (2006, 2010, 2014) raises questions about who can lay claim to ownership of communal expressive practices such as yoga. It would seem that, just as local dances as well as local products can be appropriated and "frozen" to represent to the world Turkey or First Nations, so can yoga practices that have complex and varied local heritages be subsumed into, categorized, and, potentially, "frozen" by the TKDL. Is this protection against misappropriation? Or is this hometown piracy? Such a nationalization of yoga can be compared to the nationalistic uses of Ossian for Scotland, the Kalevala for Finland, or jazz for the U.S. Equally problematic, ancient medical practices using turmeric or embodied practices such as yoga do not stop at the gates of India. Fish (2014) points out, though, that some local voices and local ways of practicing yoga in Southeast Asia both inside *and* outside India may languish unconsidered as more internationally salable dimensions of the art are "advertised."

As conservation turns to a focus on cultural continuity, legalities pertaining to heritage protection remain so complex and clumsy that consideration of their effects on particular folk communities get lost in glittering generalities. Legal dominion over folklore at any level is awkward at best, as Boatima Boateng, in *The Copyright Thing Doesn't Work Here* (2011), points out in her investigation of how Ghanaian communities attempt to manage ownership of their *adinkra* and *kente* cloth designs (31). On all levels, communal, national, global, yoga and kente cloth are disbursed with tattered affect attached and new expressivities negotiated—often at an emotional cost or financial debit to those arguably most deeply invested.

A major issue, again, is that such practices are, by definition, in constant flux. Thus, while "creative new forms" are emerging to protect local heritage, what heritage is, how it is being threatened or protected, and by which national, global, public, or private entities, is continually subject to honest confusion or acquisitive obfuscation. The efficacy of one-size-fits-all legal solutions is questionable (Fish 2014). Because folklorists are likely to have a nuanced understanding of folk and lore and the vagaries of changing socio-legal systems introduced at local levels, they can offer insights

into the ramifications of Solomonic pronouncements' unintended consequences, both affective and economic for various local communities. Work
at the interstices of folkloristics and other disciplinary resources intent on
social justice (Hufford, 2007; Feltault 2006) can, in the new digital age,
resist the new old impulse to categorize and departmentalize—what Fish
(2014: 20) refers to as the rush to "salvage and sort."

CONCLUSION

In sum, this last chapter offers some trajectories that folklorists,
or scholars who want to include folklore in their paths to understanding the human condition, can pursue. In its essence, folklore is gritty,
and folkloristics today is likely to engage with that dimension close up.
Communal affect is manifested in and powerfully informs fields only
apparently far from our own. Both global development and the knotty
problem of intellectual property rights, especially for the vulnerable,
have come increasingly within the purview of folkloristics. These
issues carry forward and coalesce around concerns—agency, inequality, exploitation, discrimination, disasters ("natural," human-made, or
both), colonialism, reification of the nation-state, or the military-industrial complex. The expanding role of folklore has opened new interests
in community engagement, culture and the environment, culture and
the economy, folk law, and institutional law.

These focuses have been in the folklorists' playbook always,
although more centrally as the urgency of paying attention to global–
local networks is widely recognized. Looking back over the past three
hundred years, we see how folklore study, with its trickster-like pro-
clivities, has been entangled with massive injustices. But folklore,
unbound, has also provided a means of pushing back—affectively and
effectively—and of learning from our diverse folk communities ways to
triumph over the thorniest problems of human beings on this planet.

Bibliography

Aarne, Antti, and Stith Thompson. 1961[1928]. *The Types of the Folktale: A Classification and Bibliography*. 2nd Revised Edition. Folklore Fellows Communications, vol. 75, no. 184. Helsinki: Suomalainen Tiedeakatemia.

Abrahams, Roger D. 1971. "Personal Power and Social Restraint in the Definition of Folklore." *Journal of American Folklore* 84: 16–30.

Abu-Lughod, Lila. 1991. "Writing Against Culture." In *Recapturing Anthropology: Working in the Present*, edited by Richard G. Fox, 137–62. Santa Fe, NM: School of American Research Press.

———. 1998. *Remaking Women: Feminism and Modernity in the Middle East*. Princeton, N.J.: Princeton University Press.

Agamben, Giorgio, and Daniel Heller-Roazen. 1998. *Homo Sacer*. Stanford, CA: Stanford University Press.

———. 2004. *State of Exception*. Translated by Kevin Attell. Chicago: University of Chicago Press.

Alvarez, Maribel. 2008. "Strike a Global Pose: Considerations for Working with Folk and Traditional Cultures in the 21st Century. Issues in Folk Arts and Traditional Culture." Working Paper Series No. 3. Austin, TX: The Fund for Folk Culture. Location: http://hdl.handle.net/2022/6595.

Alvey, R. Gerald. 1973."Phillips Barry and Anglo-American Folksong Scholarship." *Journal of the Folklore Institute* 10(1/2): 67–95.

Anagnostou, Yiorgos. 2006. "Metaethnography in the Age of 'Popular Folklore.'" *Journal of American Folklore* 119(474): 381–414.

Anderson, Jon W. 1997. "Interpretation in Middle East Ethnography: Lords of the Lebanese Marches: Violence and Narrative in an Arab Society." *American Ethnologist* 24(1): 203–7.

Anonymous. 1894. "Intelligence and Originality of Primitive Man." *Journal of American Folklore* 7(26): 250–51.

Appiah, Kwame Anthony.1991. "Is the Post- in Postmodernism the Post- in Postcolonial?" *Critical Inquiry*. 17(2): 336–57.

———. 1992. *In My Father's House: Africa in the Philosophy of Culture*. Oxford: Oxford University Press.

Armstrong, Robert Plant. 1971. *The Affecting Presence: An Essay in Humanistic Anthropology*. Urbana: University of Illinois Press.

Babcock, Barbara. 1987. "Taking Liberties, Writing from the Margins, and Doing It with a Difference." *The Journal of American folklore* 100(398): 390–411.

Barbeau, C. Marius. 1919. "The Field of European Folk-Lore in America." *Journal of American Folklore* 32(124): 185–97.

Baron, Robert, and Nick Spitzer, eds. 2007. *Public Folklore.* Jacksonville. University Press of Mississippi.

Bateson, Gregory. 1972. *Steps to an Ecology of Mind.* New York: Ballantine.

Bauman, Richard. 1972. "The La Have Island General Store: Sociability and Verbal Art in a Nova Scotia Community." *Journal of American Folklore* 85(338): 330–43.

———. 1974. "Verbal Art as Performance. Working Papers in Sociolinguistics, No. 18." Austin, TX: Southwest Educational Development Lab. Available: http://files.eric.ed.gov/fulltext/ED126692.pdf.

———. 1975. "Quaker Folk-Linguistics and Folklore." In *Approaches to Semiotics,* edited by Thomas A. Sebok. The Hague: Mouton.

———. 1983. "The Field Study of Folklore in Context." In *Handbook of American Folklore,* edited by Richard M. Dorson, 362–68. Bloomington: Indiana University Press.

———. 1984. *Verbal Art as Performance.* Long Grove, IL: Waveland Press.

———. 1986. "Performance and Honor in 13th-Century Iceland." *Journal of American Folklore* 99(392): 131–50.

Bauman, Richard, and Charles L. Briggs. 1990. "Poetics and Performance as Critical Perspectives on Language and Social Life." *Annual Review of Anthropology* 19: 59–88.

———. 2003. *Voices of Modernity: Language Ideologies and the Politics of Inequality.* Cambridge, UK: Cambridge University Press.

Bauman, Richard, and Americo Paredes, eds. 1972. *Toward New Perspectives in Folklore.* Austin: University of Texas Press.

Bauman, Richard, and Joel Sherzer. 1974. *Explorations in the Ethnography of Speaking.* London: Cambridge University Press.

Bearman, C. J.. 2002. "Cecil Sharp in Somerset: Some Reflections on the Work of David Harker." *Folklore* 113(1): 11–34

Becker, Jérôme. 1887. *La vie en Afrique, ou, Trois ans dans l'Afrique centrale.* Paris: J. Lebègue.

Ben-Amos, Dan. 1971. "Toward a Definition of Folklore in Context." *Journal of American Folklore* 84(331): 3–15.

Bennett, Gillian. 1991. "Contemporary Legend: An Insider's View." *Folklore* 102(2): 187–91.

Berger, Harris M., and Giovanna P. Del Negro. 2002. "Bauman's Verbal Art and the Social Organization of Attention: The Role of Reflexivity in the Aesthetics of Performance." *Journal of American Folklore* 115(455): 62–91.

Bernstein, Basil. 1971. *Class, Codes and Control, Vol. I: Theoretical Studies towards a Sociology of Language.* London: Routledge & Kegan Paul.

Berreman, Gerald D. 1972. "'Bringing It All Back Home': Malaise in Anthropology." In *Reinventing Anthropology,* edited by Dell Hymes, 83–98. New York: Vintage.

Bhabha, Homi K. 1994. *The Location of Culture.* London: Routledge.

Bidney, David. "Review of the New Golden Bough: A New Abridgement of the Classical Work by James George Frazer; Theodor H. Gaster." *Journal of American Folklore* 76(299):79–80.

Boas, Franz. 1894. "Notes on the Eskimo of Port Clarence, Alaska." *Journal of American Folklore* 7(26): 205–8.

———. 1901. "The Mind of Primitive Man." *Journal of American Folklore* 14(52): 1–11.

———. 1908. *Decorative Designs of Alaskan Needlecases: A Study in the History of Conventional Designs, Based on Materials in the U.S. National Museum.* Washington, DC: Government Print Office.

Boateng, Boatima. 2011. *The Copyright Thing Doesn't Work Here: Adinkra and Kente Cloth and Intellectual Property in Ghana.* Minneapolis: University of Minnesota Press.

Bock, Sheila. 2012. "Contextualization, Reflexivity, and the Study of Diabetes-Related Stigma." *Journal of Folklore Research* 49(2): 153–78.

Bock, Sheila, and Katherine Borland. 2011. "Exotic Identities: Dance, Difference, and Self-fashioning." *Journal of Folklore Research* 48(1): 1–36.

Borland, Katherine. 1991. "'That's Not What I Said': Interpretive Conflict in Oral Narrative Research." In *Women's Words: The Feminist Practice of Oral History*, edited by S. B. Gluck and D. Patai, 63–75. New York: Routledge.

Borrows, John. 1998. "Frozen Rights in Canada: Constitutional Interpretation and the Trickster." *American Indian Law Review* 22(1): 37–64.

Botkin, B. A. 1944. "Dust on the Folklorists." *Journal of American Folklore* 57(224):139.

Bourke, John G. 1893. "The Miracle Play of the Rio Grande." *Journal of American Folklore* 6(21): 89–95.

———. 1896. "Notes on the Language and Folk-Usage of the Rio Grande Valley. (With Especial Regard to Survivals of Arabic Custom.)." *Journal of American Folklore* 9(33): 81–116.

Brady, Erika. 1999. *A Spiral Way: How the Phonograph Changed Ethnography*. Jackson: University Press of Mississippi.

Briggs, Charles L. 1996. "The Politics of Discursive Authority in Research on the 'Invention of Tradition.'" *Cultural Anthropology* 11(4): 435–69.

———. 2008. "Disciplining Folkloristics." *Journal of Folklore Research* 45(1): 91–105.

Bronner, Simon J. 1983. "Review of the Powers of Presence: Consciousness, Myth, and Affecting Presence by Robert Plant Armstrong." *Journal of American Folklore* 96(381): 348–50.

———. 2002. *Folk Nation: Folklore in the Creation of American Tradition*. Wilmington, DE: Scholarly Resources.

Brooke, Charlotte. 1789. *Reliques of Irish Poetry: Consisting of Heroic Poems, Odes, Elegies, and Songs, Translated into English Verse: With Notes Explanatory and Historical; and the Originals in the Irish Character. To Which Is Subjoined an Irish Tale*. Dublin: George Bonham, printer.

Brown, Steven. 2001. "The 'Musilanguage' Model of Music Evolution." In *The Origins of Music*, edited by Nils Lennart Wallin, Björn Merker, Steven Brown, 271–300. Cambridge MA: MIT Press.

Bruner, Edward M., and Barbara Kirshenblatt-Gimblett. 1994. "Maasai on the Lawn: Tourist Realism in East Africa." *Cultural Anthropology* 9: 435–70.

Brunvand, Jan Harold. 1968. *The Study of American Folklore: An Introduction*. New York: W.W. Norton.

Burne, Charlotte Sophia. 1911. "The Essential Unity of Folklore" (Presidential Address). *Folk-Lore* 22:14–40.

Burne, Charlotte Sophia, and George Laurence Gomme. 1913. *The Handbook of Folklore*. London: Sidgwich & Jackson.

Burstein, Sona Rosa. 1957. "George Laurence Gomme and the Science of Folklore." *Folklore*. 68(2): 321–38.

Burton, Richard Francis. 1852. *Falconry in the Valley of the Indus. [With illustrations.]*. London: John Van Voorst.

———. 2001[1884–86]. *The Arabian Nights: Tales from a Thousand and One Nights*. New York and Toronto: Random House.

Buschmann, Rainer F. 2009. *Anthropology's Global Histories: the Ethnographic Frontier in German New Guinea, 1870–1935*. Honolulu: University of Hawai'i Press. Available: http://site.ebrary.com/id/10386619.

Carr, Revell. 1999. "Deadhead Tales of the Supernatural: A Folkloristic Analysis." In *Perspectives on the Grateful Dead*, edited by Robert G. Weiner, 203–12. Westport, CT: Greenwood Press.

Cashman, Ray. 2008. *Storytelling on the Northern Irish Border: Characters and Community*. Bloomington: Indiana University Press.

Catholic Truth Society (Great Britain). 1896. *Folk-Lore Ex Cathedra: Being an Examination of Mr. Edward Clodd's Presidential Address to the Folk-Lore Society, 1896*. London: Catholic Truth Society.

Çelik, İpek Azime. 2002. *Spectacular Regimes and Political Drama: A Comparative Study of Greek and Turkish Theatre in the 1960s and 1970s.* Columbus: The Ohio State University.

Clodd, Edward. 1895. "Presidential Address." *Folklore* 6(1):54–82.

———. 1896. "Presidential Address." *Folklore.* 7(1): 35–60.

Coe, Cati. 2000. "The Education of the Folk: Peasant Schools and Folklore Scholarship." *Journal of American Folklore* 113(447): 20–43.

Coffin, Tristram Potter. 1968. "Preface." In *Our Living Traditions*, edited by Tristram Coffin, v–ix. New York: Basic.

Coombe, Rosemary J. *The Cultural Life of Intellectual Properties: Authorship, Appropriation, and the Law (Post-Contemporary Interventions).* Durham, NC: Duke University Press.

Cox, Marian Roalfe. 1893. *Cinderella.* London: Folk-Lore Society.

Darányi, Sándor, and László Forró. 2012. "Detecting Multiple Motif Co-Occurrences in the Aarne-Thompson-Uther Tale Type Catalog: A Preliminary Survey." *Anales de Documentación* 15(1): 1–11. Available: http://www.redalyc.org/pdf/635/63524084003.pdf.

Darányi, Sándor, Peter Wittek, and László Forró. n.d. "Toward Sequencing 'Narrative DNA': Tale Types, Motif Strings and Memetic Pathways." Swedish School of Library and Information Science, University of Borås. Available: http://bada.hb.se/bitstream/2320/11830/2/Towards%20Sequencing%20Narrative%20DNA.pdf.

Darwin, Charles. 1963[1859]. *On the Origin of Species by Means of Natural Selection: Or, The Preservation of Favoured Races in the Struggle for Life.* New York: Heritage Press.

Delgado, Richard. 1995. "Rodrigo's Final Chronicle: Cultural Power, the Law Reviews, and the Attack on Narrative Jurisprudence." *Southern California Law Review* 68(3): 545–75.

Del Negro, Giovanna, and Harris M. Berger. 2001. "Character Divination and Kinetic Sculpture in the Central Italian Passeggiata (Ritual Promenade): Interpretive Frameworks and Expressive Practices from a Body-Centered Perspective." *Journal of American Folklore* 114(451): 5–19.

Derrida, Jacques. 1971. "La mythologie blanche (la métaphore dans le texte philosophique)." *Poétique—Revue de théorie et d'analyse littéraires* no. 5: 1–53.

Diamond, Stanley. 1974. *In Search of the Primitive: A Critique of Civilization.* New Brunswick, NJ: Transaction Publishers.

Donald, Merlin. 1991. *Origins of the Modern Mind.* Cambridge, MA: Harvard University Press.

Dorson, Richard M. 1961. "Folklore Studies in England." *The Journal of American Folklore* 74(294): 302–12.

———. 1971. *American Folklore and the Historian.* Chicago: University of Chicago Press.

———. 1983. *Handbook of American Folklore.* Bloomington: Indiana University Press.

Dorst, John D. 1983. "Neck-Riddle as a Dialogue of Genres: Applying Bakhtin's Genre Theory." *Journal of American Folklore* 96(382): 413–33.

Du Bois, William Edward Burghardt. 1903. *The Souls of Black Folk: Essays and Sketches.* Chicago: A.C. McClurg.

Dundes, Alan. 1964. "Texture, Text, and Context." *Southern Folklore Quarterly* 28: 251–65.

———. 1965a. *The Study of Folklore.* Englewood Cliffs, NJ: Prentice-Hall.

———. 1965b. "Here I Sit: A Study of American Latrinalia." *Kroeber Anthropological Society Papers* 34: 91–105. The Regents of the University of California. Available: http://digitalassets.lib.berkeley.edu/anthpubs/ucb/text/kas034-010.pdf.

———. 1972. "Folk Ideas as Units of World View." In *Toward New Perspectives in Folklore*, edited by Americo Paredes and Richard Bauman, 93–103. Austin: University of Texas Press.

———. 1978. "Into the Endzone for a Touchdown: A Psychoanalytic Consideration of American Football." *Western Folklore* 37(2): 75–88.

———. 1980. *Interpreting Folklore*. Bloomington: Indiana University Press.

———. 1980. "Who Are the Folk?" In *Interpreting Folklore*, pp. 1–19. Bloomington: Indiana University Press.

Eberhard, Wolfram, and Pertev Nailî Boratav. 1953. *Typen türkischer Volksmärchen*. Wiesbaden: F. Steiner.

Eisenstein, Elizabeth. 1979. *The Printing Press as an Agent of Change*. Cambridge, UK: Cambridge University Press.

Emrich, Duncan. 1946. "'Folk-Lore': William John Thoms." *California Folklore Quarterly* 5(4): 355–74.

Erdman, David V. 1954. *Blake, Prophet against Empire: A Poet's Interpretation of the History of His Own Times*. Princeton: Princeton University Press.

Evans-Pritchard, E. E. 1940. *The Political System of the Anuak of the Anglo-Egyptian Sudan*. London: P. Lund Humphries.

———. 1968. *The Nuer: A Description of the Modes of Livelihood and Political Institutions of a Nilotic People*. Oxford: Clarendon Press.

Fabian, Johannes. 2000. *Out of Our Minds: Reason and Madness in the Exploration of Central Africa*. Berkeley and Los Angeles: University of California Press.

Fallows, James. 2004, January 1. "Blind into Baghdad." *The Atlantic*. Available: http://www.theatlantic.com/magazine/archive/2004/01/blind-into-baghdad/302860/.

Feltault, Kelly. 2006. "Development Folklife: Human security and Cultural Conservation." *Journal of American Folklore* 119(471): 90–110.

Fenton, William N. 1962. "This Island, the World on the Turtle's Back." *Journal of American Folklore* 75(298): 283–300.

Fernandez, James W. 2002. "The Disease of Language and the Language of Disease." In *Proceedings of the British Academy*, vol. 117, *2001 Lectures*, edited by the British Academy, 355–400. London: Oxford University Press.

Fish, Allison. 2006. "The Commodification and Exchange of Knowledge in the Case of Transnational Yoga." *The International Journal of Cultural Property* 13(2): 189–206.

———. 2010. Laying Claim to Yoga: Intellectual Property, Cultural Rights, and the Digital Archive in India. PhD Dissertation, University of California, Irvine.

———. 2014. "Authorizing Yoga: The Pragmatics of Cultural Stewardship in the Digital Era." *East Asian Science, Technology and Society: An International Journal* 8: 1–23.

Fitch, W. Tecumseh. 2009, February 12. "Musical Protolanguage: Darwin's Theory of Language Evolution Revisited." *Language Log*. Available: http://languagelog.ldc.upenn.edu/nll/?p=1136.

———. 2010. *The Evolution of Language*. Cambridge: Cambridge University Press.

Foucault, Michel. 2003. *"Society Must Be Defended:" Lectures at the College De France 1975–1976*. Translated by David Macey. New York: Picador.

Frazer, James George. 1951. *The Golden Bough: A Study in Magic and Religion*. New York: Macmillan. (Several editions were published between 1890 and 1915.)

Geertz, Clifford. 1973. *The Interpretation of Cultures: Selected Essays*. New York: Basic.

Gencarella, Stephen Olbrys. 2009. "Constituting Folklore: A Case for Critical Folklore Studies." *Journal of American Folklore* 122(484): 172–96.

———. 2011. "Folk Criticism and the Art of Critical Folklore Studies." *Journal of American Folklore* 124(494): 251–71.

Georges, Robert A., and Michael Owen Jones. 1995. *Folkloristics: An Introduction*. Bloomington: Indiana University Press.

Gewen, Barry. 2008, June 11. "Who Is a Public Intellectual?" *New York Times*. Available: http://artsbeat.blogs.nytimes.com/2008/06/11/who-is-a-public-intellectual/?_php=true&_type=blogs&_r=0.

Gilman, Lisa. 2009. "Genre, Agency, and Meaning in the Analysis of Complex Performances: The Case of a Malawian Political Rally." *Journal of American Folklore* 122(485): 335–62.

Glassie, Henry. 1973. *Folk Housing in Middle Virginia: A Structural Analysis of Historic Artifacts*. Knoxville: University of Tennessee Press.

———. 1982. *Passing the Time in Ballymenone: Culture and History of an Ulster Community*. Philadelphia: University of Pennsylvania Press.

———. 1999. *Material Culture*. Bloomington: Indiana University Press.

Goffman, Erving. 1974. *Frame Analysis: An essay on the Organization of Experience*. New York: Harper & Row.

———. 1981. "The Lecture." In *Forms of Talk*, 160–96. Philadelphia: University of Pennsylvania Press.

Gomme, Alice Bertha. 1894. *The Traditional Games of England, Scotland, and Ireland, with Tunes, Singing-rhymes, and Methods of Playing according to the Variants Extant and Recorded in Different Parts of the Kingdom*. London: D. Nutt.

Gomme, G. Laurence. 1885. "The Science of Folk-Lore." *The Folk-Lore Journal* 3(1): 1–16.

———. 1893. "Annual Address by the President." *Folk-Lore* 4(1):1–26.

Goodall, Jane. 2011, July 4. "Marshall Islanders' Painful Memories of Nuclear Testing." *The Guardian*. Available: http://www.guardian.co.uk/world/2011/jul/04/nuclear-weapons-test-anniversary-fukushima.

Goody, Jack. 1977. *The Domestication of the Savage Mind*. Cambridge, UK: Cambridge University Press.

Goodyear, Sara Suleri. 1989. *Meatless Days*. Chicago: University of Chicago Press.

Gregory, Dick. 1964. *Nigger: An Autobiography*. New York: Dutton.

Gregory, Lady. 1976. *Seventy Years: Being the Autobiography of Lady Gregory*. New York: Macmillan.

Grimm, Jacob, and Wilhelm Grimm. 1962. *Kinder- und Hausmärchen*. Düsseldorf: Diederichs.

Grimm, Jacob, Wilhelm Grimm, and Wanda Gag. 1936. *Tales from Grimm*. New York: Coward-McCan.

Grimm, Jacob, Wilhelm Grimm, Jack Zipes, and Johnny Gruelle. 1987. *The Complete Fairy Tales of the Brothers Grimm*. Toronto: Bantam.

Hardy, Thomas. 2006 (1895). *Jude the Obscure*. Mineola, NY: Dover Publications.

Harries, Jeanette. 1973. "Pattern and Choice in Berber Weaving and Poetry." *Research in African Literatures* 4(2): 141–53.

Hartland, Edwin Sidney. 1904. *Folklore, What Is It and What Is the Good of It*. London: D. Nutt.

Hassan, Ihab. 1987. *The Postmodern Turn: Essays in Postmodern Theory and Culture*. Columbus: Ohio State University Press.

Hathaway, Rosemary V. 2005. "'Life in the TV': The Visual Nature of 9/11 Lore and Its Impact on Vernacular Response." *Journal of Folklore Research* 42(1): 33–56.

Hawes, Bess Lomax, 1974. "Folksongs and Function: Some Thoughts on the American Lullaby." *Journal of American Folklore* 87(344): 140–48.

Hemenway, Robert E. 1977. *Zora Neale Hurston: A Literary Biography*. Urbana: University of Illinois Press.

Henkes, Barbara, and Richard Johnson. 2002. "Silences across Disciplines: Folklore Studies, Cultural Studies, and History." *Journal of Folklore Research* 3(2/3): 125–46.

Hewitt, J. N. B. 1974. *Iroquoian Cosmology*. New York: AMS Press.

Hickey, Dave. 1997. "Romancing the Looky-Loos." In *Air Guitar: Essays on Art & Democracy*, 146–54. Los Angeles: Art Issues Press.

Hicks, Dan. 2010. "The Material-Cultural Turn: Event and Effect." In *The Oxford Handbook of Material Culture Studies*, edited by Dan Hicks and Mary C. Beaudry, 25–98. Oxford: Oxford University Press.

Hufford, Mary. 1991. *American Folklife: A Commonwealth of Cultures*. Washington DC: American Folklife Center, Library of Congress. Available: http://www.loc.gov/folklife/cwc/CWCbooklet.pdf.

———. 2003. "Context." In *Eight Words for the Study of Expressive Culture*, edited by Burt Feintuch, 146–75. Urbana: University of Illinois Press.

Hufford, Mary, with Thomas Carroll, Rita Moonsammy, Linda Lee, Cynthia Byrd, and Dana Hercbergs. 2007. *Ethnographic Overview and Assessment: New River Gorge National River and Gauley River National Recreation Area*. Prepared under cooperative agreement with: The Center for Folklore and Ethnography, University of Pennsylvania, and Northeast Region Ethnography Program, National Park Service, Boston, MA. Washington, DC: U.S. Department of the Interior. Available: http://www.sas.upenn.edu/folklore/center/NGR_report_final.pdf.

Hughes, Langston. 1940. *The Big Sea: An Autobiography*. New York: Alfred A. Knopf.

Huntington, Samuel P. 2004. *Who Are We?: The Challenges to America's National Identity*. New York: Simon & Schuster.

Hurston, Zora Neale. 1935. *Mules and Men*. New York: Harper & Row.

———. 2008. *Mules and Men*. New York: HarperCollins.

Hymes, Dell. 1975. "Breakthrough into Performance." In *Folklore: Performance and Communication*, edited by Dan Ben-Amos and Kenneth S. Goldstein, 11–74. The Hague & Paris: Mouton.

———. 1979. "Review of *In Search of the Primitive. A Critique of Civilization*." *Journal of American Folklore* 92(366): 491–92.

———. 2004. *"In Vain I Tried to Tell You": Essays in Native American Ethnopoetics*. Omaha: University of Nebraska Press.

Irai, Saritha. 2001, August 25. "India–U.S. Fight on Basmati Rice Is Mostly Settled." *The New York Times*. Available: http://www.nytimes.com/2001/08/25/business/india-us-fight-on-basmati-rice-is-mostly-settled.html.

Jackson, Jason Baird. 2013. "The Story of Colonialism, or Rethinking the Ox-Hide Purchase in Native North America and Beyond." *Journal of American Folklore* 126(499): 31–54.

Jacobs, Joseph. 1893. "The Folk." *Folk-Lore* 4: 233–38.

Jacobs, Joseph, Alfred Trübner Nutt, Arthur Robinson Wright, and William Crooke. 1890. *Folklore*. London: Folklore Society.

Kapchan, Deborah A. 1996. *Gender on the Market: Moroccan Women and the Revoicing of Tradition*. Philadelphia: University of Pennsylvania Press.

———. 1994. "Moroccan Female Performers Defining the Social Body." *Journal of American Folklore* 107(423): 82–105.

———. 1995. "Performance." *Journal of American Folklore* 108(430): 479–508.

———. 2003. "Performance." In *Eight Words for the Study of Expressive Culture*, edited by Burt Feintuch, 112–45. Urbana: University of Illinois Press.

Kaufman, King. 2003, January 8. "Football: America's Favorite Homoerotic Sport." *Salon.com*.

Kirshenblatt-Gimblett, Barbara. 1988. "Mistaken Dichotomies." *Journal of American Folklore* 101(400): 140–55.

Kissane, James. 1962. "Victorian Mythology." *Victorian Studies* 6(1): 5–28.

Korotayev, Andrey, Yuri Berezkin, Artem Kozmin, and Alexandra Arkhipova. 2006. "Return of the White Raven: Postdiluvial Reconnaissance Motif A2234.1.1 Reconsidered." *Journal of American Folklore* 119(472): 203–35.

Korson, George Gershon. 1943. *Coal Dust on the Fiddle: Songs and Stories of the Bituminous Industry*. Philadelphia: University of Pennsylvania Press.

Kuhn, Thomas S. 2012[1962]. *The Structure of Scientific Revolutions*. Chicago: University of Chicago Press.

Kiupers, Giselinde. 2006. *Good Humor, Bad Taste: A Sociology of the Joke*, translated by Kate Simms. Berlin: Walter de Gruyter.

Kurin, Richard. 2004, October. "Brokering the Intangible: The Art of Cultural Brokerage." *Diversity: Arts in a Multicultural Australia*. Available: http://www.australiacouncil.gov.au/__data/assets/pdf_file/0011/3800/Diversity_2004_oct.pdf.

Lane, Edward William. 1902. *An Account of the Manners and Customs of the Modern Egyptians: Written in Egypt During the Years 1833–1835*. London, New York: Ward, Lock.

Leerssen, Joseph T. 2004a. "Literary Historicism: Romanticism, Philologists, and the Presence of the Past." *MLQ: Modern Language Quarterly* 65(2): 221–43.

———. 2004b. "Ossian and the Rise of Literary Historicism." In *The Reception of Ossian in Europe*, edited by Howard Gaskil, 109–25. London: Thoemmes Continuum.

Lévi-Strauss, Claude. 1964. *Le cru et le cuit*. Paris: Plon.

———. 1966. *Du miel aux cendres*. Paris: Plon.

———. 1972. *The Savage Mind (La pensée sauvage)*. London: Weidenfeld and Nicolson.

———. 1978. *The Origin of Table Manners (L'Origine des manières de table)*. New York: Harper & Row.

———. 1981. *The Naked Man: (L'homme nu)*. New York: Harper & Row.

Lévy-Bruhl, Lucien. 1966[1927]. *The "Soul" of the Primitive*. New York: Praeger.

Liberman, Anatoly. 2008. "William John Thoms, The Man Who Invented The Word Folklore." OUP Blog. http://blog.oup.com/2008/07/folklore/.

Lillios, Anna. 2010. *Crossing the Creek: The Literary Friendship of Zora Neale Hurston and Marjorie Kinnan Rawlings*. Gainesville: University Press of Florida.

Lindahl, C. 2010. "Leonard Roberts, The Farmer-Lewis-Muncy Family, and the Magic Circle of the Mountain Märchen" *Journal of American Folklore* 123(489): 251–75.

———. 2012. "Legends of Hurricane Katrina: The Right to Be Wrong, Survivor-to-Survivor Storytelling and Healing." *Journal of American Folklore* 125(496): 139–76.

Littledale, R. F. 1906. "The Oxford Solar Myth." In *Echoes from Kottabos*, edited by R. Y. Tyrrell and Sir Edward Sullivan, 279–90. London: E. Grant Richards.

Lönnrot, Elias, and Francis Peabody Magoun. 1963. *The Kalevala; or, Poems of the Kaleva District*. Cambridge, MA: Harvard University Press.

Lowie, Robert H. 1917. "Oral Tradition and History." *Journal of American Folklore* 30(116): 161–67.

MacCraith, Micheal. 2004. "'We know all these poems': The Irish Response to Ossian." In *The Reception of Ossian in Europe*, edited by Howard Gaskill. London: Thoemmes Continuum.

Macpherson, James, and Hugh Blair. 1846. *The Poems of Ossian*. New York: E. Kearny.

Malinowski, Bronislaw. 1948. *Magic, Science and Religion: and other essays*. New York: Dutton. Long Grove, IL: Waveland Press, 2013.

Manjapra, Kris. 2013. "The Work of Comparison: Contact, Relation, Entanglements." Second workshop in the "Comparison as Method" series, Columbus, The Ohio State University, March 4.

Masuzawa, Tomoko. 1993. *In Search of Dreamtime: The Quest for the Origin of Religion*. Chicago: University of Chicago Press.

———. 2003. "Our Master's Voice: Friedrich Max Müller after a Hundred Years of Solitude." *Method and Theory in the Study of Religion* 15(4): 305–28.

McArthur, Phillip H. 2008. "Ambivalent Fantasies: Local Prehistories and Global Dramas in the Marshall Islands." *Journal of Folklore Research* 45(3): 263–98.

Mechling, Jay. 1986. "Children's Folklore." In *Folk Groups and Folk Genres: An Introduction*, edited by Elliott Oring, 91–120. Logan: Utah State University Press.

Mercer, Kobena. 1994. *Welcome to the Jungle: New Positions in Black Cultural Studies*. New York: Routledge.

Moore, Erin. 1990. "Dream Bread: An Exemplum in a Rajasthani Panchayat." *Journal of American Folklore* 103(409): 301–23.

Mullen, Patrick B. 1996. "On Being a Folklorist in an English Department: Implications for Research." *Journal of Folklore Research* 33(1): 48–55.

Müller, F. Max. 1861. *Lectures on the Science of Language*. Oxford: Oxford University Press.

———. 1862. *Lectures on the Science of Language*. London: Longman, Green, Longman and Roberts

———. 1897. *Contributions to the Science of Mythology*. London, New York, and Bombay: Longmans, Green.

———. 1901. *My Autobiography: A Fragment*. New York: Charles Scribner's Sons.

Müller, F. Max, and Sastri K. A. Nilakanta. 1961. *India, What Can It Teach Us?* Delhi: Munshi Ram Manohar Lal.

Nader, Laura 1974[1969]. "Up the Anthropologist—Perspectives Gained From Studying Up." In *Reinventing Anthropology*, edited by Dell Hymes, 284–311. New York: Vintage.

Naithani, Sadhana. 2004. "Colonial Hegemony and Oral Discourse." *Indian Folklife* 3(2): 10.

Newell, William Wells. 1888. "English Folk-Tales in America I." *Journal of American Folklore* 1(3): 227–34.

Noyes, Dorothy. 1993. "Review of Living in a Material World: Canadian and American Approaches to Material Culture by Gerald R. Pocius." *Journal of American Folklore* 106(421): 347–49.

———. 1995. "Group." *Journal of American Folklore* 108(430): 449–78.

———. 2006. "The Judgment of Solomon: Global Protections for Tradition and the Problem of Community Ownership." *Cultural Analysis* 5: 27–56.

O'Brien, Karen. 2002. "Poetry Against Empire: Milton to Shelley." In *Proceedings of the British Academy*, vol. 117: *2001 Lectures*, edited by British Academy, 269–96. London: Oxford University Press.

Odum, Howard W. 1911a. "Folk-Song and Folk-Poetry as Found in the Secular Songs of the Southern Negroes." *The Journal of American Folklore* 24(93): 255–294.

———. 1911b. "Folk-Song and Folk-Poetry as Found in the Secular Songs of the Southern Negroes (Concluded)." *The Journal of American Folklore* 24(94): 351–396.

Odum, Howard Washington, and Guy Benton Johnson. 1925. *The Negro and His Songs: A Study of Typical Negro Songs in the South*. Chapel Hill: University of North Carolina Press.

Orchard, William C. 1916. *The Technique of Porcupine-Quill Decoration among the North American Indians*. New York: Museum of the American Indian, Heye Foundation.

Oring, Elliott 1986. "Folk Narratives." In *Folk Groups and Folk Genres: An Introduction*, edited by Elliott Oring, 121–43. Logan: Utah State University Press.

O'Rourke, Dennis. 1985. *Half-Life: A Parable for the Nuclear Age*. Australian documentary. 86 minutes. Distributed by Kino International.

Öztürkmen, Arzu. 2005. "Folklore on Trial: Pertev Naili Boratav and the Denationalization of Turkish Folklore." *Journal of Folklore Research* 42(2): 185–216.

Paredes, Américo, and Richard Bauman, eds. 1972. *Toward New Perspectives in Folklore*. Austin: University of Texas Press.

Pax, Salam. 2003. *Salam Pax: The Clandestine Diary of an Ordinary Iraqi*. London: Atlantic Books. (Blog: http://salampax.wordpress.com/2003/02/)

Penny, H. Glenn. 2003. "Bastian's Museum: On the Limits of Empiricism and the Transformation of German Ethnology." In *Worldly Provincialism: German Anthropology in the Age of Empire*, edited by H. Penny and M. Bunzl, 86–126. Ann Arbor: University of Michigan Press.

Penny, Simon. 2008. "Bridging Two Cultures: Towards an Interdisciplinary History of the Artist-Inventor and the Machine-Artwork." In *Artists as Inventors-Inventors as Artists*, edited by Dieter Daniels and Barbara U. Schmidt, 142–57. Ostfildern, Germany: Hatje Cantz Verlag.

Pound, Ezra. 1914. "Vorticism." *Fortnightly Review* 96 [n.s.], 1: 461–71. Available: http://fortnightlyreview.co.uk/vorticism/.

Pratt, Mary Louise. 1986. "Fieldwork in Common Places." In *Writing Culture: The Poetics and Politics of Ethnography: A School of American Research Advanced Seminar*, edited by James Clifford and George E. Marcus, 27–50. Berkeley: University of California Press.

———. 1992. *Imperial Eyes: Travel Writing and Transculturation*. London: Routledge.

Propp, Vladimir. 2008. *Morphology of the Folktale*. Austin: University of Texas Press.

Quiller-Couch, Arthur Thomas, Sir. 1908. *The Oxford Book of English Verse: 1250–1900*. Oxford: Clarendon Press.

Raponda-Walker, André. 1993. *Souvenirs d'un nonagenaire*. Versailles, France: Les Classiques Africains.

Reuss, Richard A. 1974. "'That Can't Be Alan Dundes! Alan Dundes Is Taller than That!': The Folklore of Folklorists." *Journal of American Folklore* 87(346): 303–17.

Reynolds, Dwight. 1995. *Heroic Poets, Poetic Heroes: The Ethnography of Performance in an Arabic Oral Epic Tradition*. Ithaca: Cornell University Press.

———— (ed). 2007. *Arab Folklore: A Handbook*. Westport, CT: Greenwood Press.

Rikoon J. 2004. "On the Politics of the Politics of Origins: Social (In)Justice and the International Agenda on Intellectual Property, Traditional Knowledge, and Folklore." *Journal of American Folklore* 117(465): 325–36.

Rooth, Anna Birgitta. 1962. *The Raven and the Carcass: An Investigation of a Motif in the Deluge Myth in Europe, Asia, and North America*. Helsinki: Suomalainen Tiedeakatemia.

Ruxin, Paul T., Lord Alexander Boswell Auchinleck, Samuel Johnson, and James Boswell. 2004. *Lord Auchinleck's Fingal: Being Remarks Inscribed in the Hand of Alexander Boswell in His Own Copy of James Macpherson's Ossian Offerings, with an Introductory Essay on the Johnson/Macpherson Controversy*, translated by James Macpherson. New Haven, CT: Yale University.

Said, Edward W. 1989. "Representing the Colonized: Anthropology's Interlocutors." *Critical Inquiry* 15(2): 205–25.

Salih, Tayeb. 1969[1966]. *Season of Migration to the North*. London: Heinemann.

Sanford, Rikoon J. 2004. "American Folklore Society Recommendations to the WIPO Intergovernmental Committee on Intellectual Property and Genetic Resources, Traditional Knowledge, and Folklore." *Journal of American Folklore* 117(465): 296–99.

Schlereth, Thomas J. 1982. *Material Culture Studies in America*. Nashville, TN: American Association for State and Local History.

Scott, James C. 1976. *The Moral Economy of the Peasant: Rebellion and Subsistence in Southeast Asia*. New Haven: Yale University Press.

————. 1985. *Weapons of the Weak: Everyday Forms of Peasant Resistance*. New Haven: Yale University Press.

————. 1990. *Domination and the Arts of Resistance: Hidden Transcripts*. New Haven: Yale University Press.

————. 2009. *The Art of Not Being Governed*. New Haven, CT: Yale University Press.

Sims, Martha C., and Martine Stephens. 2005. *Living Folklore: An Introduction to the Study of People and Their Traditions*. Logan: Utah State University Press.

Slyomovics, Susan. 1998. *The Object of Memory: Arab and Jew Narrate the Palestinian Village*. Philadelphia: University of Pennsylvania Press.

Small, Christopher. 1994. "Whose Music Do We Teach Anyway?" *Muse Letter* 2: 4–9.

Spargo, John W. 1944. "Review of George Korson's *Coal Dust on the Fiddle*." *Journal of American Folklore* 57(223): 91–92.

Stocking, George. 1987. *Victorian Anthropology*. New York: The Free Press.

Stoeltje, Beverly J. 1988. "Gender Representations in Performance: The Cowgirl and the Hostess." *Journal of Folklore Research* 25(3): 219–41.

Strathern, Marilyn. 1992. "Reproducing Anthropology." In *Contemporary Futures: Perspectives from Social Anthropology*, edited by Sandra Wallman, 172–89. London: Routledge.

Suleri, Sarah. 1989. *Meatless Days*. Chicago: University of Chicago Press.

Sunder, Madhavi. 2012. *From Goods to a Good Life: Intellectual Property and Global Justice*. New Haven, CT: Yale University Press.

Swann-Jones, Steven. 1995. *The Fairy Tale: The Magic Mirror of the Imagination*. New York: Twayne Publishers.

Thomas, Nicholas. 1991. *Entangled Objects: Exchange, Material Culture, and Colonialism in the Pacific*. Cambridge: Harvard University Press.

Thomas, Northcote Whitridge, comp. 1906. *Bibliography of Folk-Lore, 1905.* London: D. Nutt.

———, comp. 1908. *Bibliography of Anthropology and Folk-Lore, 1907.* London: Royal Anthropological Institute.

Thompson, Stith. 1960[1932–36]. *Motif-Index of Folk-Literature,* 6 volumes. Bloomington: Indiana University Press.

Thoms, William J. 1996[1846]. "'Folk-Lore,' from *The Athenæum,* August 22, 1846." *Journal of Folklore Research* 33(3): 187–89.

Toelken, Barre. 1979. *The Dynamics of Folklore.* Boston: Houghton Mifflin.

———. 1998. "The End of Folklore: The 1998 Archer Taylor Memorial Lecture." *Western Folklore* 57(2/3): 81–101.

Tooker, Elisabeth, and Barbara Graymont. 2007. "J.N.B. Hewitt." *Histories of Anthropology Annual* 3(1): 70–98.

Trubshaw, Bob. 2002. *Explore Folklore.* Loughborough, UK: Heart of Albion Press.

Tylor, Edward B. 1924. *Primitive Culture: Researches into the Development of Mythology, Philosophy, Religion, Language, Art, and Custom.* New York: Brentano's.

Uther, Hans-Jörg. 2004. *The Types of International Folktales: A Classification and Bibliography, Based on the System of Antti Aarne and Stith Thompson.* Helsinki: Suomalainen Tiedeakatemia, Academia Scientiarum Fennica.

Utley, Francis Lee. 1953. "Three Kinds of Honesty." *Journal of American Folklore* 66(261): 189–99.

Vlach, John Michael. 1995. "Fred B. Kniffen's Milestones in American Folklife Study." *The Journal of American Folklore* 108(429): 328–33.

Wade, Nicholas. 2010. "Anthropology a Science? Statement Deepens a Rift" *New York Times,* December 9. Available: http://www.nytimes.com/2010/12/10/science/10anthropology.html?_r=0.

Walters, Keith. 1999. "'He Can Read My Writing but He Sho' Can't Read My Mind' Zora Neale Hurston's Revenge in *Mules and Men.*" *Journal of American Folklore* 112(445): 343–71.

Weber, Max. 1996. *The Protestant Ethic and the Spirit of Capitalism.* Los Angeles: Roxbury.

Webber, Sabra Jean. 1991. *Romancing the Real: Folklore and Ethnographic Representation in North Africa.* Philadelphia: University of Pennsylvania Press.

Webber, Sabra J., and Patrick B. Mullen. 2011. "Breakthrough into Comparison: 'Moving' Stories, Local History, and the Narrative Turn." *Journal of Folklore Research* 48(3): 213–47.

Williams, Raymond. 1977. *Marxism and Literature.* Oxford: Oxford University Press.

———. 2001. *The Long Revolution.* Peterborough, Ontario: Broadview Press.

Wordsworth, William. 1804[1940]. *The Poetical Works of William Wordsworth.* Oxford: Clarendon Press.

Wright, Thomas. 1906. *The Life of Sir Richard Burton.* London: Everett.

Zeitler, Michael A. 2007. *Representations of Culture: Thomas Hardy's Wessex & Victorian Anthropology.* New York: Peter Lang.

Zeitlin, Steven J. 2000. "I'm a Folklorist and You're Not." *Journal of American Folklore* 113(447): 3–19.

Zumwalt, Rosemary Lévy. 1988. *American Folklore Scholarship: A Dialogue of Dissent.* Bloomington: Indiana University Press.

Index